MW01672897

FRESHWATER FISHES

Dr. Herbert R. Axelrod

BOOK 1

This book is dedicated to my father, Dr. Aaron Axelrod. He was the first author in our family.

Throughout the text various parts of a fish's anatomy are referred to which might not be familiar to the novice. A typical fish, *Prochilodus insignis* from Brazil, has been selected as our model. Some fishes might have additional characteristics which this characin does not have, such as a second dorsal fin or barbels. The code used in the overlay above is as follows: **1** = mouth; **2** = dorsal fin; **3** = adipose fin; **4** = tail fin; **5** = caudal peduncle; **6** = anal fin; **7** = ventral fin, of which there are two; **8** = pectoral fin, of which there are two; **9** = gill cover or opercle; **0** = eye. The tail fin is sometimes referred to as the caudal fin.

ISBN 0-87666-076-6

©1974 by T.F.H. Publications, Inc. Ltd.

Distributed in the U.S.A. by T.F.H. Publications, Inc., 211 West Sylvania Avenue, P.O. Box 27, Neptune City, N.J. 07753; in England by T.F.H. (Gt. Britain) Ltd., 13 Nutley Lane, Reigate, Surrey; in Canada to the book store and library trade by Clarke, Irwin & Company, Clarwin House, 791 St. Clair Avenue West, Toronto 10, Ontario; in Canada to the pet trade by Rolf C. Hagen Ltd., 3225 Sartelon Street, Montreal 382, Quebec; in Southeast Asia by Y.W. Ong, 9 Lorong 36 Geylang, Singapore 14; in Australia and the south Pacific by Pet Imports Pty. Ltd., P.O. Box 149, Brookvale 2100, N.S.W., Australia. Published by T.F.H. Publications Inc. Ltd., The British Crown Colony of Hong Kong.

CATFISHES p. 260

LIVEBEARERS p. 274

ODD-BALLS p. 294

CHARACINS p. 9

CYPRINIDS p. 94

CICHLIDS p. 196

ANABANTOIDS p. 162

INTRODUCTION

Every book is supposed to have a purpose; or, at least, it must have a reason for being written. This book has several purposes, and it has been written for several reasons. I am writing this INTRODUCTION as the last bit of written work I have to do for the completion of the book, since the objectives (reasons and purposes) have changed in the last few years this book has been under construction.

One of the main reasons I decided to write this book was to show the world what made fishes so interesting for me. I was introduced to fishes by Dr. Myron Gordon when we were using them as laboratory animals delving into the intricacies of human cancer problems. Fishes are subject to cancer, and since we could breed several generations of them in one year we hoped to find out what caused the cancer, how cancer was (or was not) passed on from one generation to the next and, if possible, how it might be controlled. In certain types of cancer we could actually predict with almost 100% accuracy how many and what kinds of cancer would appear on our fishes. We also found that by breeding certain fishes together we would or would not get cancer. We were not able to inhibit the growth of cancer in fishes once it started, though the untimely death of Myron Gordon certainly cut short this most important direction of our research. The cancer we studied was the type referred to as carcinoma. Because the cancer we developed in our fishes was basically "made" in our laboratory, we often had to collect swordtails and platyfishes in the wild to verify certain observations and get new populations for further experimentation. On many of these collecting trips we found fishes other than those which we were looking for, and I discovered that almost none of these "other" fishes had ever been photographed alive or even printed in a book with suitable color drawings which might make their identification more simple.

That started me writing books and using photographs and drawings extensively. The rewards of writing were sufficient stimulation to keep me going

A black wagtail swordtail would have a black dorsal fin. This fish does not have such a dorsal and if you look closely you can observe that just as the tail fin begins at the back, dorsal edge, a slight rise indicates an abnormality. This fish is cancerous and will develop a melanoma. Dr. Myron Gordon (right) developed the red jet swordtail below which was a non-cancerous strain.

Two of the world's greatest fish photographers who have helped the author considerably are Rudolf Zukal (photo taken in 1971) of Brno, Czechoslovakia in the upper photo and Hans Joachim Richter (1971 photo below) of Leipzig, DDR Germany.

and, since my first book written in 1949, I have completed almost 100 books to date! You would think that in these many books I would have said everything there is to say about fishes. Far from it!

There are 20,000 or more fishes in the world. Perhaps I know 10% of them from having collected them and photographed them alive. And of these 20,000 how many have been photographed spawning? How many have been observed courting. . . or feeding. . . and how many new fishes have never even been catalogued???

So this book will, I hope, be the first in a long series of books which will show, with detailed color photography, some of the secrets and beauty of fishes including, but not limited to, their color variations, their reproductive and social life, where and how they live in their native habitat, and perhaps some tips on how to keep them alive in the home aquarium.

Many of the photographs which appear in this series will have appeared before in *Tropical Fish Hobbyist* magazine, because as I learn some of these secrets, I publish them to finance new expeditions to find more new fishes and to learn more about the old finny friends I have. But most of the photographs will be new to most of the readers of this book and, thanks to a wonderful cooperation with some of the world's outstanding fish photographers like Hans Joachim Richter of Leipzig, East Germany and Rudolf Zukal of Brno, Czechoslovakia, I am able to present the spawning habits of many of these fishes.

I have also written a series of books on the breeding of aquarium fishes (*Breeding Aquarium Fishes* Books 1, 2 and 3 have been published to date). These books go into great detail in both words and pictures about how fishes spawn. I hope to continue that series of books quite separately from this series, for that series is for the aquarist or professional interested in breeding his fishes.

This series is for the person just interested in fishes. He doesn't have to be an aquarist to appreciate nature, but I hope that the stimulation he receives will prompt him to at least visit an aquarium shop and see some of the beauty swimming about in the tanks. So you can see that another purpose of this book is to stimulate nature lovers to be aquarists.

It's too soon to know how this book will be received, but if it goes well I'd like to produce one volume every year for as many years as I'm able to pry into our fishes' many secrets.

I cannot take full credit for this book. While I did all the writing and made all the nomenclatural decisions, these decisions were based upon substantial help from the scientific community as well as the editorial staff of T.F.H. I also have to thank many of the fish breeders and fish collectors around the world who have acted as guides in the jungle, have loaned me their boats and nets, and who even have given me their only specimens of very rare fishes so I could photograph them and then preserve them for scientific study. Just a few weeks ago Jack Freiberg, an importer of African fishes, brought in a new species for which he refused $150 for a single pair. I photographed them and asked if I could preserve the fish in formalin so I could study it. He gulped a little and bravely gave me permission. As I put the sleeping fish into preservative I could swear Jack's eyes were a bit moist. . . not because of the money, but because *he* had found this new fish. When it is named in his honor and appears in the next book in this series, I hope his dedication to the hobby and the science of fish-keeping will have been rewarded.

This book deviates from all the normal presentations of past fish books. There is, basically, no scientific order to the book. Instead I grouped the fishes according to the classifications on the price lists of most aquarium fish wholesalers. If that's the way they sell their fishes, maybe that's the way I should write about them.

Rudolf Zukal set up an aquarium exhibit in Brno, Czechoslovakia in 1973 to show how to decorate various types of aquariums for home decoration. These are two photographs showing each side of the room, but they have been joined together for effect in these excellent Zukal photographs.

THE CHARACINS OR

Characins may be the most popular of all aquarium

TETRAS

fishes; they certainly are the most colorful and easy to keep.

Blackline tetras, *Hyphessobrycon scholzei*. Photo by Dr. Herbert R. Axelrod.

THE CHARACINS OR TETRAS

With the possible exception of the freshwater clupeids (herring and anchovy-like fishes) found in the great lakes of Africa, characins are by far the most numerous fishes found in the freshwaters of Africa and South America. Even Central America has its fair share of these usually smaller fishes, with at least one species getting into Texas. So, basically, the tetras are the fodder fishes upon which the larger fishes subsist.

For the poorer peoples of the bush, tetras are also useful as they are caught easily and plentifully and are used to flavor the otherwise tasteless manioc and rice diets upon which many of these less fortunate peoples depend.

Since tetras are so easily caught, they are usually the least expensive of many of our aquarium fishes, for basically they are school fishes and when they are found, they are usually found in large numbers. So plentiful are they in most of South America's small streams, that I have often been prevented from bathing in shallow streams because thousands of tiny tetras would attack me as I rinsed the soap from my body. I say "attack" in the literal sense, since tiny characins hardly do more than pinch the skin as they attempt to pick off whatever skin flakes they can manage to tear loose with their tiny, sharp teeth. No blood is ever drawn, but the experience is most uncomfortable. Compare it to being covered with thousands of flies.

Not all tetras are small. . . and certainly not all are peaceful. The deadly piranhas of South America, while not the bloodthirsty beasts that many writers portray, still are equipped to tear huge chunks of flesh from whatever they decide to attack. I have bathed in

The photos above and below depict the "bloodthirsty" piranhas of the freshwaters of South America. While they have the teeth to tear almost any living animal apart, they have never been known to attack anything but a dying or bleeding fish or mammal, except in cases where they are under severe stress, such as a dessicating lake. Photos by Dr. Herbert R. Axelrod.

waters very rich in piranhas and I swam with many natives who showed no fear of piranhas, even though I had caught dozens of them only minutes before. My experience with piranhas is that they will not attack humans or animals unless these animals are dead and decaying or unless the piranhas are in a very unnatural situation. Such situations are, for example, reservoirs which are drying out and the piranhas are starving, or when they are trapped in seines and are in a panic state. However, I would *never* stick my hand into a tank with even one piranha in it, and I quite agree with various laws which prohibit the importation or display of piranhas in home aquaria.

But along with the nasty tetras, there are the very beautiful ones. Could there be anything more beautiful than the tiny neon tetras, *Paracheirodon. innesi*? Or the larger and more popular cardinal tetra, *Cheirodon axelrodi*? To say nothing of all the gorgeous *Hemigrammus* and *Hyphessobrycon* species. But the accompanying photographs speak for themselves, so let's look at how these beautiful fishes are differentiated from others and how they live in their natural habitats.

What is a characin or tetra?

A characin or tetra is a very fish-like fish. It is usually greater in depth than in thickness and has a streamlined appearance. ALL of them have teeth and scales and NONE of them has barbels or whiskers. MANY of them have an extra fin on the top, rear of their body which is called an adipose fin; this fin has no spines or rays. They are not found in Europe, Asia or Australia, nor in North America (except for Texas). There are about 1,500 known species with at least another few hundred waiting to be discovered in Africa and South America. Most of them eat everything, preferring living foods such as other fishes, aquatic insects and worms; but some prefer plant foods and algae. In the aquarium almost all the smaller tetras will eat dry foods, though they must be fed live foods if they are to really show off their beautiful colors and be brought to spawning condition.

How characins breed

All characins lay eggs; mostly the eggs are haphazardly sprayed wherever an interesting clump of plants are found. In nature their spawning mainly coincides with the beginning of the rainy season, but in the aquarium they spawn all year round. With but few exceptions, most of the males have longer dorsal and anal fins, and in some genera the males are more highly colored, especially during breeding time.

The best way to spawn tetras is to separate the males from the females, feed them heavily on live foods until the females grow fat and the males get more colorful, and then introduce them into a specially prepared spawning tank which has clean, aged water in which clumps of fine-leaved plants have been strategically placed. The techniques for each fish may vary slightly, but most eat their eggs almost as quickly as they lay them. Consult any of a number of good books on breeding aquarium fishes and get all the details of the particular fish in which you are interested.

How do characins live in nature?

I have found hundreds of different species of characins in South America and Africa. It is almost impossible to find any clean, unpolluted body of water which does not have tetras in it. Yet the most beautiful of tetras are found in very special places and these habitats have many common characteristics. First, colorful tetras seem to prefer shaded, very clean, slow moving streams. The shading can come from a dense, overhead growth of trees, or, more rarely, by plants covering the surface of the water. The water is usually not too deep, perhaps as shallow as one foot and not more than ten feet. The water is almost always acid and is usually cooler by 10 to 20° than the highest air temperature. Coincidentally, perhaps, I have always found colorful tetras where there were plenty of palm trees near the water.

Since tetras are usually very fast swimmers, no matter how hard one tries to catch them all, many always escape even the best netting efforts

There are some fishes which are easily confused with the dreaded piranhas of South America and these are fishes of the genera *Metynnis* and *Mylossoma*. In the wild these fishes are usually found in the same open rivers as the piranhas, but they are usually vegetarians. Because they are so tasty and easily caught in open waters, they are a favorite food fish and are very common amongst the daily catches of the native fishermen in the jungle. The upper fish is *Metynnis hypsauchen*; the lower fish is an immature *Mylossoma* species. Photos by Dr. Herbert R. Axelrod.

and, as a result, no tetra has ever disappeared from its range by being overfished. At least 50,000,000 neons and cardinals are caught every year in Brazil, Colombia and Peru. As soon as their numbers are depleted and further fishing is economically unsound in a given area, they easily reproduce during the next highwater season and are as plentiful as they were before.

Aquarium fishes are one of the truly replenishable natural resources of such countries as Malawi, Zaire, Tanganyika, Brazil, Guyana, Colombia, Peru and other areas from which tetras are exported. What destroys populations of fishes are not the fishermen, but the poisonous discharge of mining and lumber operations now springing up in remote jungle areas.

Serrasalmus hollandi.

Serrasalmus nattereri.

Serrasalmus nattereri.

Serrasalmus niger.

Several countries have already banned the importation of the piranha, not because there has ever been a case of any piranha ever becoming established outside of South America, but only because the authorities are afraid of someone being accidentally bitten. Unfortunately for the authorities, piranhas are being spawned and raised in sufficient quantities to supply the marketplace. The fish left, above is *Serrasalmus hollandi*, a rare species which has not yet been spawned. The fish right above and lower left is *Serrasalmus nattereri*, one of the most commonly bred piranhas. Photos by Dr. Herbert R. Axelrod.

Pygocentrus piraya.

Below: A head-on view of the black piranha, *Serrasalmus niger*. Photo by Harald Schultz. Right, top to bottom: There are, perhaps, a dozen genera of fishes which have general characteristics similar to those of the piranha, except for their teeth. Each of these genera have their own characteristics, but the depth of the operculum in terms of the size of the eye is a good gauge. The deeper the operculum, the more dangerous the fish.

No, it's not real! This is a close-up view of a dead, dried piranha, the kind usually sold at most South American airports as tourist souvenirs. The value of the photo is that the teeth are real and resemble shark's teeth in their pointed sharpness. Photo by Dr. Herbert R. Axelrod.

Myleus asterias is a very beautiful fish which is very plentiful in the black water rivers in the kingdom of the neon tetra. Photo by Harald Schultz.

A juvenile *Myloplus* (?) species. This new fish has never been accurately identified. Photo by Dr. Herbert R. Axelrod.

Mylossoma argenteum, sometimes called *Mylossoma duriventre*. Photo by Hans Joachim Franke.

Characins in your aquarium

Since characins are school fishes, they do best in schools in your home aquarium. The ideal situation is a school of a single species of fish in a tank well planted around the back and sides, with plenty of free swimming room in the center. However, most aquarists are hardly ever content with just one species of fish, though just for pure contentment a 20 gallon, well filtered aquarium with 50 cardinal tetras and a Gro-lux type fluorescent fixture lighting the tank from above, rivals anything I have ever experienced.

Basically all tetras of the same size get along together fairly well if they are well fed and not crowded. . . and tetras can easily be crowded for they are very hardy. It is not difficult to keep 200 cardinal tetras in the same heavily aerated and filtered 20 gallon aquarium, but they would not thrive. A better idea is to allow about 5 inches of fish per gallon of water; thus 100 inches of tetras would be the maximum for a 20 gallon aquarium, assuming proper aeration and filtration.

Metynnis hypsauchen has a black edge on its tail fin which resembles the coloration of some piranhas, often being confused with these fishes. Actually *Metynnis hypsauchen* is a vegetable eater. Photo by Dr. Herbert R. Axelrod.

This is a new species of piranha which grows larger than any the author has ever seen. A specimen almost two feet long has been deposited at the Smithsonian Institution waiting for someone to describe it; another 18 inch specimen decorates the wall in the author's study. The fish shown in this photo (being held by a Brazilian indian) is the one in the Smithsonian. Photo by Harald Schultz.

Metynnis luna is a very rarely seen pacu from Brazilian waters. Photo by Dr. Herbert R. Axelrod.

This fish has been misidentified by many experts and aquarists since it appeared in a fish calendar some years ago. Originally the fish was described as *Metynnis schreitmuelleri*, then it was later called *Metynnis hypsauchen*. Unfortunately, without the fish itself to examine I am unable to make a decision as to what it should be called. Photo by Kremser.

Tetras are fast eaters, so never feed them more than they will eat in three minutes. Its best to feed them several times a day and as long as they gobble up their food in three minutes you are not overfeeding. NO FISH WILL OVEREAT; overfed tanks become polluted because the fish do not eat the food offered and the uneaten food falls to the bottom where it soon rots. No filtering system can take an endless overfeeding situation.

While tetras get along pretty well with other tetras, they usually do not get along with slow-moving fishes such as fishes with long, trailing fins like angelfish (*Pterophyllum*) or gouramis. They can be kept with other fast moving fishes like barbs, danios and rasboras, and such sedentary scavengers as most small catfish (*Corydoras*, are best) but be sure the catfish have small mouths. Most catfish are nocturnal and can gobble up small tetras during the night while they are resting. I have even had luck with small goldfish as scavengers in a large tetra tank!

Udo Loew, Harald Schultz's assistant, shows a sample piranha catch, in the upper left hand photograph. On the bottom left is another catch. Note that piranhas are, more or less, the same size within each catch. The center left photograph shows a vicious-looking piranha on display in the Berlin (Germany) Aquarium. Photo by H. Hansen.

A new species of *Metynnis*, as yet unidentified. Photo by Dr. Herbert R. Axelrod.

Many of the juvenile fishes we collect are difficult to identify since the early scientists only used large nets in open waters, thus restricting their catch mainly to mature adult *Metynnis*. I collected mainly in small ditches where the aquarium fishes hide, thus my collection is mainly juveniles of the river fishes. The upper fish is an unidentified spotted *Metynnis*; the photo below shows a juvenile *Myleus rubripinnis* which may be a synonym of *M. asterias*. Photos by Dr. Herbert R. Axelrod.

Metynnis maculatus.

A close-up of the head of *Mylossoma duriventre* showing the lack of visible teeth.

A juvenile *Myloplus* showing protective coloration. Photo by Dr. Herbert R. Axelrod.

Myloplus schomburgki, an adult, probably a male. Photo by Dr. Herbert R. Axelrod.

The Rio Purus as seen from the town of Tapaua. In this town are to be found beautiful discus, colorful neons, and several different kinds of *Metynnis, Myloplus* and piranhas. Photo by Dr. Herbert R. Axelrod.

A juvenile *Myleus* species. Photo by Dr. Herbert R. Axelrod.

Myleus rubripinnis, the red metynnis. Photo by Dr. Herbert R. Axelrod.

Pencilfishes, metynnis and piranhas are all characins. The largest of the so-called "pencilfishes," is also the most popular. *Anostomus anostomus* is sold by the millions every year but they have never been spawned in a home aquarium. Photo by Dr. Herbert R. Axelrod.

The long, slender fishes of several pencilfish genera are closely related. The upper fish is an *Anostomus* species; the center fish is *Laemolyta varia*; while the lower fish is a *Leporinus*. Photos by Dr. Herbert R. Axelrod.

This is a so-called "pair" of *Anostomus anostomus*. The female, the lower fish, is supposedly fuller than the male and there is a visible difference in color. Since no one has spawned these fishes in their aquarium, it is very difficult to sex the fishes for certain by coloration. Photo by Dr. Herbert R. Axelrod.

Closely related to *Anostomus anostomus* is *Anostomus trimaculatus*, the silver anostomus, or 3-spot anostomus (whose scientific name is still unverified). Photo by Dr. Herbert R. Axelrod.

Prochilodus taeniurus is a common food fish throughout its range in Brazil. Small specimens are usually available only in late November at the end of the dry season. Photo by Dr. Herbert R. Axelrod.

A very rare pencilfish is *Apareidon pongoensis* which scoots around at the bottom of the tank swimming in circles so it can stir up the small organisms on the bottom and eat them with their tiny mouths. Photo by Dr. Herbert R. Axelrod.

Nannostomus trimaculatus is a very common pencilfish found in a small stream similar to that shown in this village of the Tukuna indians in Brazil. Photos by Dr. Herbert R. Axelrod.

Nannostomus anomalus spawning among the fine-leaved plants. The fish rub against each other and spray their eggs in a very haphazard manner. Photo by Rudi Zukal.

Another *Anostomus* which is supposed to be *A. trimaculatus*. Photo by H. Hansen at the Berlin Aquarium.

A long, slender fish which resembles a pencilfish but which has sharp teeth and eats other fishes is *Phago maculatus*. Photo by Klaus Paysan.

Poecilobrycon diagrammus is a very rarely seen pencilfish from the Rio Madeira in central Brazil. It lacks the color found in most pencilfishes. Photo by Dr. Herbert R. Axelrod.

A much more colorful and, consequently, more popular pencilfish is *Poecilobrycon unifasciatus*. This fish normally swims at a 45° angle. Photo by Harald Schultz of fish just collected in the Brazilian jungle.

Poecilobrycon eques is a very common pencilfish which is both imported and bred in quantities. The female is the fish which is more full. Photo of a spawning pair by Rudolf Zukal.

A closer view of a spawning pair of *Poecilobrycon eques*. These fish actually spawned within minutes of the taking of this photograph. When selecting fishes for spawning it is always wise to select the fullest female and the most active and colorful male available. Photo by Hans Joachim Richter.

The male *Nannostomus marginatus*, a very small and beautiful pencilfish, is the upper fish in this photograph. The female heads for the plants in order to release her eggs where they will be protected by the bushy vegetation.

The male follows the female to the vegetation so he can fertilize her eggs as she releases them.

(Facing page) *Nannostomus marginatus* spawning. This head-on view shows the different thickness of the two sexes and how the fishes line up their bodies against one another during the spawning process to insure the fertilization of their eggs. This series of photographs by Hans Joachim Richter.

Then, in a side by side motion, the *Nannostomus marginatus* push and rub against each other as the eggs are released. Photo by Hans Joachim Richter.

A male *Nannostomus anomalus* in full breeding color. Some tank-raised varieties are completely suffused with red during spawning. The photograph below shows a plump female *Nannostomus anomalus* ready for spawning. Photos by Hans Joachim Richter.

A male *Nannostomus anomalus* chasing a ripe female into the vegetation in order to spawn with her. Pencilfish have small mouths and require very fine foods. Newly hatched brine shrimp is considered as the ideal food with which to condition pencilfishes. Photo by Hans Joachim Richter.

A pair of *Poecilobrycon espei*, a pencilfish discovered about 1956 by Louis Chung in Guyana and named in honor of Heinrich Espe. These pencilfish were always rare and considered very difficult to breed. Photo by Hans Joachim Richter.

Hans Joachim Richter may have been the first person in the world to spawn (in 1973) these fish, *Poecilobrycon espei*. This photograph shows the pair diving amongst the vegetation spraying their tiny clear eggs. Photo by Hans Joachim Richter.

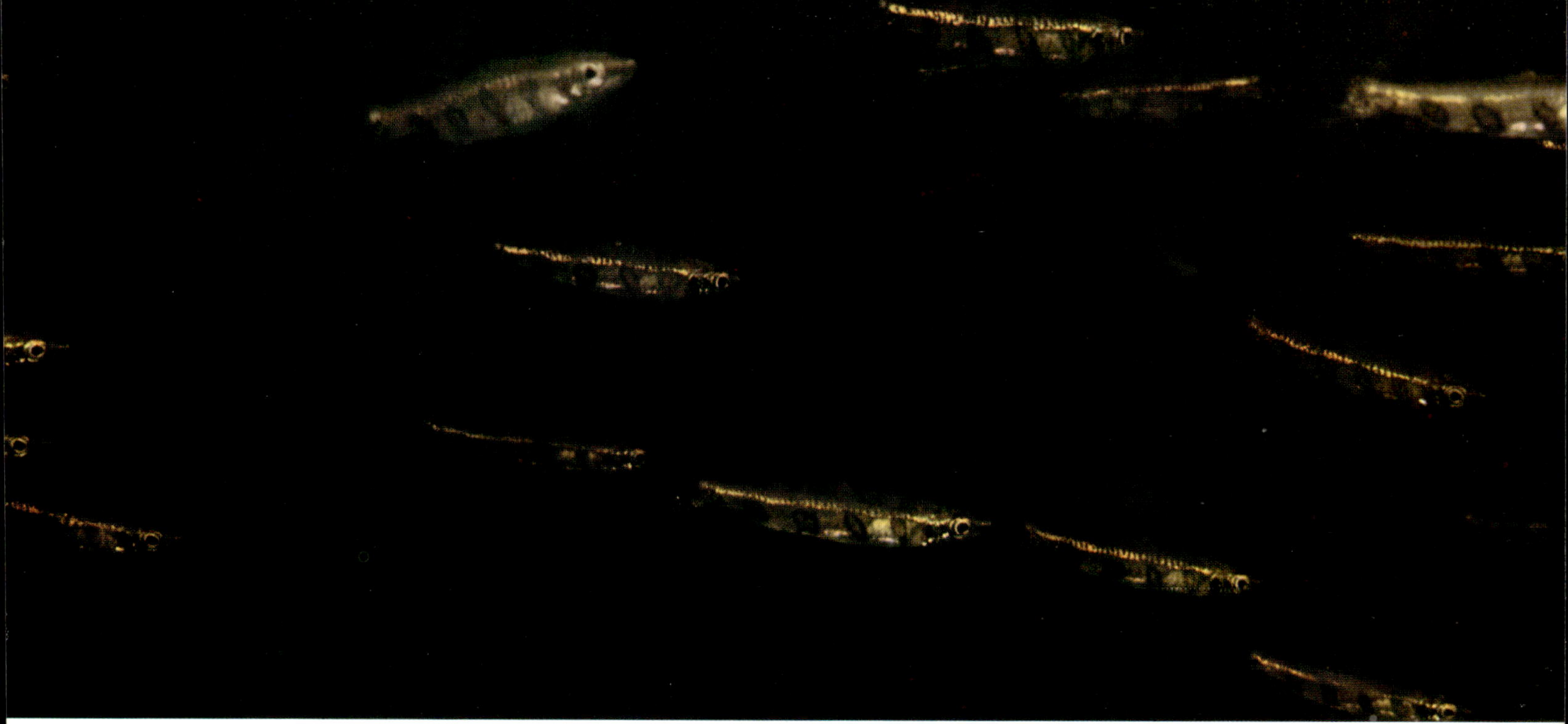

Underwater in their natural habitat in Guyana the pencilfish *Poecilobrycon espei* have a beautiful golden stripe which quickly fades in captivity. Photo by Dr. Herbert R. Axelrod.

A handsome pair of *Poecilobrycon espei*, tank-raised, and posing under the leaf of a Madagascar lace plant which propagates from a bulb or tuber. Photo by Hans Joachim Richter.

Hans Joachim Richter of Leipzig, East Germany is famous for his excellent photographs. . . but he should be credited with spawning some of the most difficult to spawn fishes as well. His series on the spawning of the pencilfish *Poecilobrycon eques* was published in many countries and in many languages. The graphic requirements of a good spawning article for a magazine are good photographs showing typical activity and a clear photograph showing the intimate characteristics of the spawning pair. This Richter does in great fashion on this page and on the facing page.

Poecilobrycon eques spawning. Photos by Hans Joachim Richter.

A pair of *Copeina guttata*. Unfortunately this pair of fish did not spawn, so their sex is not known for certain. Photo by Dr. Herbert R. Axelrod.

The genus *Leporinus* is similar in many ways to the genera of pencilfishes except for their size. Their small mouths and torpedo shape indicate they are hard to feed and they jump well! These spotted beauties are *Leporinus maculatus*, a very rare (in nature) species which is being spawned in Japan. Photo by Dr. Herbert R. Axelrod.

From the Brazilian great plains (known as the Mato Grosso) comes this striking *Leporinus striatus*, which was first described by Dr. Kner in 1859. Photo by Dr. Herbert R. Axelrod.

Leporinus pellegrini is a very rarely seen "cigar fish," a name suggested but never popularized. Photo by Dr. Herbert R. Axelrod.

This fish was also identified as *Leporinus maculatus* by an "expert." But a close comparison with the photo on top of the facing page will show this fish to be stubbier and thicker-bodied. Photo by Dr. Herbert R. Axelrod.

Leporinus fasciatus is the most widely distributed member of the genus *Leporinus*. They reach almost two feet in length and are a common food fish. Bloch first described these fish in 1795! Photo by Dr. Herbert R. Axelrod.

This is a new (or at least unidentified) species of *Leporinus*. It rarely is imported and, like all other *Leporinus*, comes from South America, east of the Andes. Photo by Dr. Herbert R. Axelrod.

There are characins that stand on their tails, like many of the pencilfishes, and then there are some fishes which stand on their heads like fishes of the genera *Abramites* and *Chilodus*. The fish to the right are *Abramites microcephalus*. The lower fish is probably the male, though these fish have never been spawned. Photo by Dr. Herbert R. Axelrod.

Another very popular headstander is *Chilodus punctatus* from South America. These fish are widespread and found with different markings in different areas. Photo by Kremser.

While the author was collecting in Puerto Gaitan, Colombia, where he found cardinal tetras in Colombia for the first time, he also found this fish which closely resembles *Chilodus* (see facing page). The name of this species is *Caenotropus labyrinthicus*. Photo by the author.

Abramites hypselonotus differs from the almost identically colored *Abramites microcephalus* by the head shape and thickness of the body compared to its length. Photo by Dr. Herbert R. Axelrod.

The similarity of some fishes is astounding. Certainly *Leporinus affinis* looks quite a bit like *Leporinus fasciatus* (see page 43) and only the thickness of the black bands gives any sure indication that any difference exists at all! Photo by Rudolf Zukal.

Characidium fasciatum is sometimes mistaken for juvenile *Leporinus affinis* or *Leporinus fasciatus*, but they are very different in other ways besides size. Photo by Dr. Herbert R. Axelrod.

Look-alikes are not limited to South America. Two very desirable aquarium fishes from Africa are *Distichodus sexfasciatus*, shown to the right, and *Distichodus lusosso*, shown below.

Distichodus lusosso was irregularly sent out of the Congo while the Belgians were in control, but as Africa discouraged participation by Europeans in their industry, especially the management of natural resources, the trickle of rare beauties from central Africa has all but stopped. Photo by Dr. Herbert R. Axelrod.

Distichodus notospilus. Photo by Dr. Jacques Gery.

Distichodus notospilus juvenile. The fish to the left is an adult. Photo by Dr. Jacques Gery.

On page 47 we showed a 12-inch long *Distichodus lusosso*. The fish shown here was photographed by the author in Africa in 1969 and is 5 inches long.

This is a small species of African characin, *Distichodus decemmaculatus*. Photo by Aaron Norman.

This is a South American fish which acts similar to *Distichodus* from Africa. This may be *Curimata spilurus*. Photo by Dr. Herbert R. Axelrod.

This unidentified *Curimatus* was collected by the author in the Rio Aguara, Venezuela. The black spots on the fins are cysts of parasites. Photo by the author.

Neolebias unitaeniatus, a very common African characin.

The Stanley Pool outside of Kinshasa (Leopodville), Zaire. At one time Pierre Brichard shipped thousands. . . maybe millions. . . of fishes every year from the renewable resources of this huge pool on the Congo River. Now that most of the Europeans have left the Congo area, almost nothing is shipped. Photo by Dr. Herbert R. Axelrod.

These two photographs show the magnificent Congo tetras which are collected in the dense vegetation found in some parts of the Stanley Pool. The top fish in this photograph is *Phenacogrammus interruptus*; the lower fish in this photograph is a very rare Congo fish of the genus *Alestopetersius*, sometimes called *A. caudalus*. Photo by Dr. Herbert R. Axelrod.

Two males and one female *Phenacogrammus interruptus*. Photo by Kremser.

Chalceus erythrurus is a rare but welcome characin from South America. Photo by Paysan.

The typical large scales sometimes confuse this species from Africa, *Arnoldichthys spilopterus*, with the South American genus *Chalceus*. Photo by Dr. Herbert R. Axelrod.

Some tetras (characins) have extensions growing from the middle of their caudal (tail) fins. *Alestopetersius caudalus* shown here is an example of an African Congo tetra showing such an extension. Photo by Dr. Herbert R. Axelrod.

Nematobrycon amphiloxus is from western Colombia in South America. These fish also have an extension coming from the center of their tails. Photo by Dr. Herbert R. Axelrod.

Nematobrycon amphiloxus. These fish were collected by the author and William Kyburz on the western slopes of Colombia in the Calima valley. I first brought them back about 1964 and I predicted they would be easily spawned and that further importations would not be necessary! How wrong I was! No one is spawning them in commercial quantities at the time of this writing (1974). Photo by the author.

These were the original *Nematobrycon palmeri* collected alive and brought back from Colombia by the author. They are being bred commercially all over the world, quite in contrast to the *N. amphiloxus*! Photo by the author.

A pair of *Nematobrycon palmeri* spawning. Photo by Hans Joachim Richter.

Carnegiella vesca, the marbled hatchetfish, is one of the most popular of Guyana's characins. It is exported by the hundreds of thousands every year. Photo by Dr. Herbert R. Axelrod.

Pristigaster cayana looks very much like a hatchetfish. This is not a characin but a herring!! It lives in the Amazon River in large schools and is a forage fish, that is, other fishes feed upon it. This fish lives on plankton and dies almost as soon as it is collected. Photo by Dr. Herbert R. Axelrod.

The rare *Thoracocharax stellatus*, the silver hatchetfish. Photo by Dr. Herbert R. Axelrod.

Thoracocharax securis. Photo by Klaus Paysan.

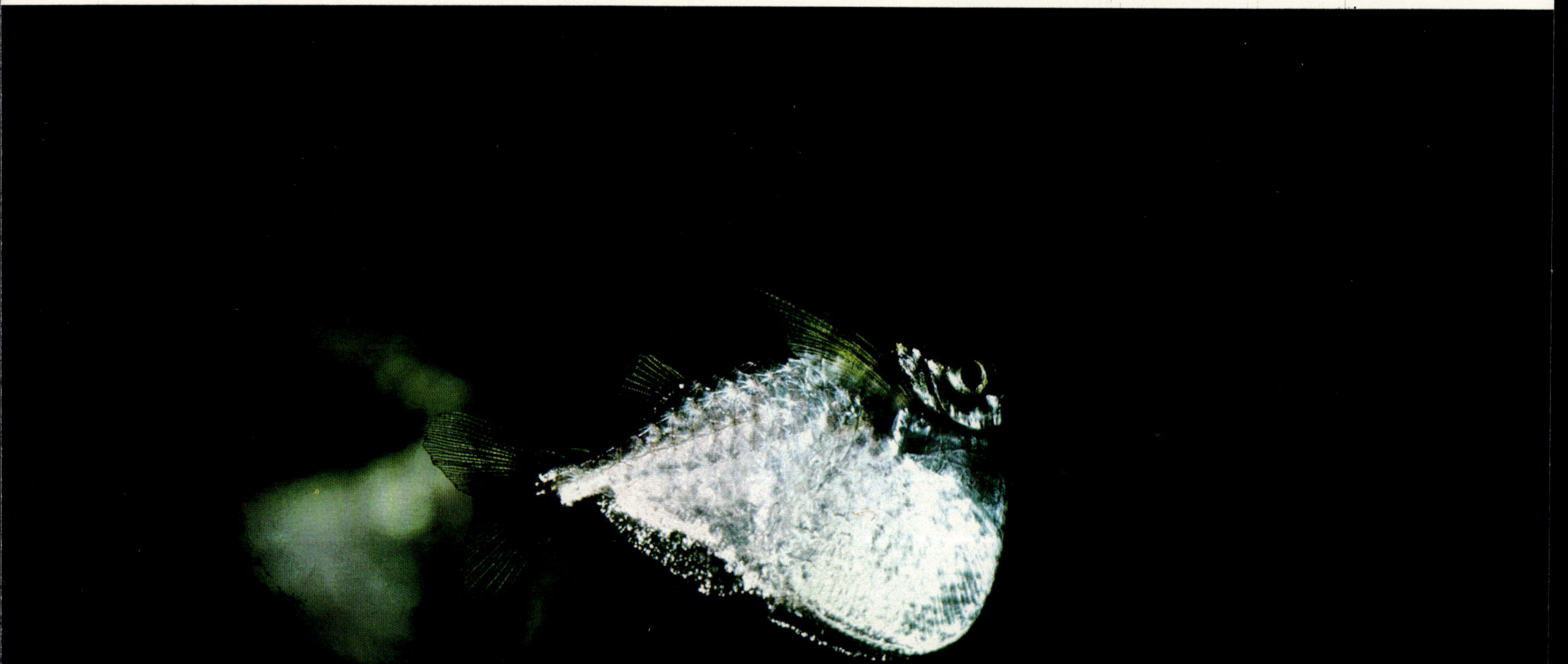

This closeup and the trio below are the usual silver hatchetfish, *Carnegiella marthae*, which range all over northern South America. This fish was described by the famous American ichthyologist Dr. George Myers in 1927 and named in honor of his wife Martha. Myers' interest in characins of South America was passed on to his student Dr. Stanley Weitzman, who assisted in the identification of many fishes in this book. Photos by Dr. Herbert R. Axelrod.

Triportheus elongatus has almost the same northern range as *Carnegiella marthae*, though its southern range into the lower Amazon extends farther south. This is not a true hatchetfish, but it is interesting and has great leaping abilities. Photo by Dr. Herbert R. Axelrod.

The various neons. . . or cardinal tetras. . . of the Amazon River system of South America are very good-selling aquarium fishes. The so-called "green neon" was the most recent discovery. It was named *Hyphessobrycon simulans* by Dr. Jacques Gery. A pair are shown here as photographed by Hans W. Peter.

A pair of spawning neon tetras, *Paracheirodon innesi*, named by Dr. George Myers to honor the late William T. Innes.

The top and third from the top fish are neon tetras, *Paracheirodon innesi*; the second from the top and bottom fish are cardinal tetras, *Cheirodon axelrodi*. Photo by Dr. Herbert R. Axelrod.

In 1965 there were about 7,500 Tukuna indians living in the territory of the range of the neon tetra. The Tukuna take certain trees and by hammering the inner bark they are able to make a cloth which they decorate with beautiful drawings. This Indian has used the neon tetra to decorate this rug. Photo by Harald Schultz.

A breeding pair of neon tetras, *Paracheirodon innesi*. Photo by Stanislav Frank.

Cardinal tetras, *Cheirodon axelrodi*, as they appear under Gro-lux fluorescent lamps. The Gro-lux lamps bring out the blues and red and have a purple hue. The fish are about 2 inches long. Photo by Dr. Herbert R. Axelrod.

A perfect setting!! This huge aquarium port-holed by a frame with a circular window contains only cardinal tetras, *Cheirodon axelrodi*. These fish were named in honor of the author by Dr. Leonard P. Schultz, who was then Curator of fishes at the Smithsonian Institution. This aquarium was photographed by Dr. Terver in Nancy, France.

Cardinal tetras (also on facing page) attacking a feeding bell containing freeze-dried tubifex worms. Freeze-dried worms and all other freeze-dried foods are excellent for most aquarium fishes. The photo above shows the fish attacking the worms. On the facing page their bloated bellies and the empty feeding bell tell the story. Photos by Dr. Herbert R. Axelrod.

I have been collecting fishes in jungles all over the world since about 1950 when I collected Siamese fighting fishes outside a military airport in Thailand. On my first Brazilian trip in the mid-1950's we were after neons and discus. We usually took a crew of four with us. One crew member would be the captain or pilot, one was a cook, one an engineer and one a fisherman. All, however, could easily substitute for the others and all loved to fish.

Our goal was usually a small stream or lake that emptied into the mighty Amazon. We never fished in the Amazon itself. This is the typical entrance to an unnamed inland lake which was always filled with many millions of aquarium fishes.

Typically we would sleep in hammocks under lean-to-type huts. But as we used larger and larger boats, we eventually preferred sleeping on board and sailing 24 hours a day.

When we would set up camp we would load all of our supplies on the beach, usually on a raft, since sudden rains in November and December might make the river rise ten feet overnight.

In the good old days (the 1950-1969 period) we used empty 5-gallon cans with doors cut in their tops. Each can would hold several hundred neons or cardinals.

The cans would then be loaded into the boat and one man would continually be adding water and siphoning as we returned to Manaus from wherever we were. This often led to huge casualties since neons come from water quite different than the Amazon muddy brown!

In 1974 I took this boat, the *Ebenezer*, from Manaus to Tefe. The trip was about 500 miles and it took 5 days or about 110 hours. Going back took only 37 hours due to the strong current. The photo shows me bathing in the Rio Tefe near Capivara, Brazil. I stayed in the water to keep the flies and mosquitoes from eating me alive!

Again we find a beautiful igarape and an inland lake which was the home of the green discus. We often dive amongst the trees and weeds to see what fishes are living there, but since this was March and the waters were high and muddy, visibility was very limited.

Photos by Dr. Martin Brittan.

Small streams like this one usually have the interesting fishes. Similar streams have cardinals and neons. Here we are seen inspecting a fish trap (the sticks in the water are a crude cage).

In Lake Tefe, I started diving around sunken tree trunks looking for discus. The local population came out to see what we were doing. I use a special mask which has glass on the sides as well as the front so I can keep my eyes open for piranhas!

As we collected the fishes, using local people as our guides to the small inland pools which almost always had lots of *Corydoras* and *Dianema* species, we put them into stackable non-toxic plastic cans.

These plastic cans could be floated on the water in order to keep them cool, or we would pour their contents into a large fish trap in the river. The trap was made of plastic mesh and could hold 50,000 neons, cardinals or *Corydoras*. This trap happened to have 60 green discus!

Dr. Martin Brittan on board the *Ebenezer* injecting fishes with formalin. The fishes we collected for study were preserved in formalin. The larger fishes, such as the *Leporinus frederici* and *L. fasciatus* in the plastic container in the foreground, would be injected with formalin so their internal organs would not decay. Photo by the author.

In the Calima area in 1974 we went searching for new *Nematobrycon* species. The roads were good, so we took a taxi. Small plastic bags were used to hold the different types of fishes we found.

Heiko Bleher is shown assisting me.

I then put the fish into a small photo tank and, utilizing the top of the taxi, took photographs of the new fishes we found. Photos by Dr. Martin Brittan.

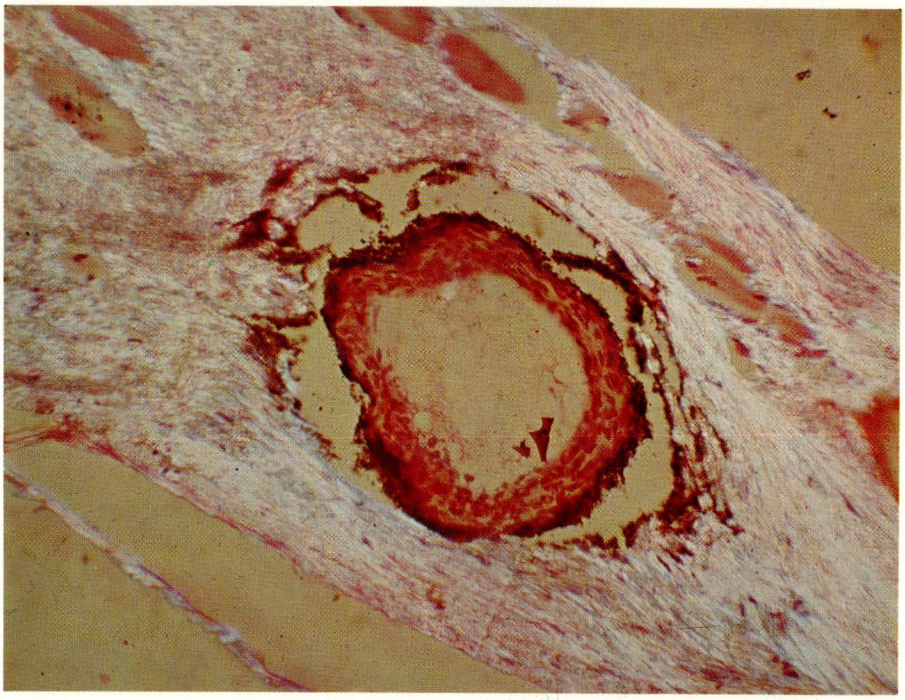

For many years no one knew why gold tetras, *Hemigrammus armstrongi*, were gold in nature whereas their offspring would always be silver. Then Dr. Jacques Gery, a physician as well as a specialist in characins, isolated a metacercarian cyst. The cyst was protected by a coating of guanin which gave the fish its golden color. Photo by Dr. Ginsburger.

The gold tetra, *Hemigrammus armstrongi*, gets its color from the cyst of a parasite. They look their best in dark, reflected light against a dark background. This photograph successfully shows them at their glistening best. Photo by the author.

One of the silver-tipped tetras, *Hemigrammus marginatus*, from South America. Photo by Stanislav Frank.

The head-and-tail light tetra, *Hemigrammus ocellifer*. Photo by Dr. Stanislav Frank.

The glowlight tetras are very popular. They are known scientificially as *Hemigrammus gracilis*. The lower fish, the more slender of the two, is the male. Photo by Rudolf Zukal.

Hyphessobrycon peruvianus. Photo by Dr. Stanislav Frank.

Petitella georgiae, the rummy-nosed tetra. The upper fish is more slender and thus the male. Dr. Jacques Gery named this species in honor of his wife, Georgi. Photo by Dr. Stanislav Frank.

Hemigrammus caudovittatus is no longer imported but is bred by the millions in the Far East, especially Hong Kong. Photo of a young pair by Rudolf Zukal.

Hyphessobrycon georgettae, named by Dr. Jacques Gery in honor of his wife, Georgette, also affectionately known as Georgi. Photo by Dr. Stanislav Frank.

A pair of *Hyphessobrycon rosaceus*. The male, the upper fish, has longer and more pointed anal and dorsal fins. Photo by Dr. Stanislav Frank.

The black neon, *Hyphessobrycon herbertaxelrodi*, named in honor of the author. Photo by Dr. Herbert R. Axelrod.

Hemigrammus gracilis, the glowlight tetra. Photo by Klaus Paysan.

Harald Schultz discovered this rare tetra in the Mato Grosso of Brazil. It was named (after a Japanese-Brazilian aquarist) *Hyphessobrycon takasei*. Photo by Harald Schultz.

A spawning pair of lemon tetras, *Hyphessobrycon pulchripinnis*. The male normally has longer anal and dorsal fins. Photo by Rudolf Zukal.

A breeding pair of *Hyphessobrycon herbertaxelrodi*. These fish are bred in huge quantities and every year their quality disintegrates. Compare these fish with the original wild strain I brought in some years ago (see page 75). Photo by Rudolf Zukal.

Hyphessobrycon heterorhabdus. The upper fish is the female. Photo by Dr. Stanislav Frank.

This *Hyphessobrycon heterorhabdus* was spotted by the author in a school of normal fish near Belem, Brazil. After capturing the specimen it was ascertained that the golden coloration was due to a similar metacercarian cyst which colors the gold tetra, *Hemigrammus armstrongi*. Photo by the author.

Hyphessobrycon agulha, which are similar to *Hyphessobrycon heterorhabdus*, occurs with the neon tetra and is found far up the Amazon in Peru. Photo by Harald Schultz.

The bleeding heart tetra, *Hyphessobrycon rubrostigma*, isn't above causing trouble by nipping the fins of its tankmates, but it's not a killer. Generally considered hardy enough, but some individuals get choosy about what they'll accept as food. It was called the "bleeding heart tetra" because of the red spot on the side. Photo by H.J. Richter.

One of the problem fishes for both the breeder, the fish shipper and the scientist is *Hyphessobrycon serpae*. No one seems to know for sure which fish is really "*serpae*".

Rudolf Zukal took this series of photographs of the fish as they were spawning. If you look very closely you can see a very faint spot on the shoulder of the fish.

A comparison of the male and female shows the male (the deeper colored fish) to have a solid black dorsal fin while the female does not. Photos in this series by Rudolf Zukal, who called them *Hyphessobrycon serpae*. The correct identification is still to be verified.

Hyphessobrycon flammeus, the tetra from Rio, has been so highly inbred that the fish being offered in pet shops look almost nothing like the original fish described by Dr. George Myers in 1924. The fish is supposed to have two dark bars where the one elongated spot shows on this pair, and the anal fin is supposed to have a black leading edge and tip. Thus the fish shown above might not even be a "real" *H. flammeus*, but it will be the fish you'll get at your pet shop under that name. Photo by Rudolf Zukal.

There is a large group of aquarium fishes which have been thoroughly confused as to their identification almost from the moment of their introduction to the aquarium trade. Basically they are all similar in form and color to *Hyphessobrycon serpae*; they have been given various names including, but not limited to, *H. serpae, H. callistus* and *H. bentosi*. The fish shown to the right are known as *Hyphessobrycon callistus bentosi* because the shoulder spot is so weak. Photo by Dr. Stanislav Frank.

These fish are called *Hyphessobrycon callistus serpae*; they are not imported fishes but have been tank-raised from previously tank-raised fishes. I doubt that anyone can ascertain what this species is. Photo by Dr. Stanislav Frank.

This is another of the "*callistus*" group and is scientificially known as *Hyphessobrycon* (*callistus*) *rosaceus*, the rosy tetra. Normally in *H. rosaceus* the males have much longer anal and dorsal fins. The two fish in this photograph cannot be sexed. Photo by Dr. Stanislav Frank.

Hyphessobrycon griemi was originally described by the Dutch ichthyologist Hoedeman in 1957 to honor Herr Griem, the proprietor of a well-known aquarium importing business known as Aquarium Hamburg (Germany). The fish is found near Goias, Brazil. Photo by Rudolf Zukal.

A beautiful male *Megalamphodus megalopterus* in breeding color dances in front of a female with his fins fully expanded. Tiny, almost invisible (to aquarists) differences in teeth are highly significant in the classification of characins; though fishes may look alike, if their teeth are different, they are often placed into different genera. Photo by Hans Joachim Richter.

Not all tetras are highly colorful, but this is truly a "tetra," which is a contraction of its scientific name *Tetragonopterus argenteus*. Photo by Dr. Herbert R. Axelrod.

Aphyocharax axelrodi, the red calypso tetra from Trinidad, was discovered by the author in a small pool near the airport. Photo by the author.

Moenkhausia oligolepis. Photo by Rudolf Zukal.

Corynopoma riisei was described by Gill in 1858. This fish ranges over Trinidad and northern Venezuela and, while it is hardy and interesting, its lack of color deters it from being very popular. This egglaying species has peculiar methods of reproduction, including internal fertilization. Photo by Rudolf Zukal.

Sardines, herrings and many open-water fishes which feed on plankton are almost impossible to maintain in captivity; so many silver fishes which are elongate just cannot be kept in a tank. Just why these herrings and related fishes are shaped this way generally is unknown, but undoubtedly evolution of the most fit shapes has led to development in this fashion. For the aquarist, this may be the closest he can come to a long, slender silver fish. It is *Aphyocharax erythrurus*. Photo by the author.

Moenkhausia pittieri is another silver fish with glistening mirror-like scales. It comes from South America. Photo by the author.

An immature *Astyanax bimaculatus* collected by the author at the Rio Aguaro, Venezuela. Photo by the author.

Fully grown *Astyanax bimaculatus* from northern South America. These are very common "silver tetras". They, or fishes which look very similar and are closely related, are found in almost every clear running stream in northern South America. They attack bathers in huge schools, gently picking at the bathers' skin and giving them an uncomfortable, though not painful, sensation. Photo by Dr. Herbert R. Axelrod.

Millions of years ago the common ancestor of *Astyanax mexicanus* and the blind cave characin, *Anoptichthys jordani* (shown to the left), was trapped in an underground pool in Mexico. They evolved into the blind cave fish while the normal fish known as the Mexican tetra developed in a normal manner. Photo by Dr. Herbert R. Axelrod.

Two females of tank-raised *Thayeria boehlkei*. Photo by Rudolf Zukal.

The penguin or hockeystick, *Thayeria boehlkei*, was referred to as *Thayeria obliqua* for many years. Finally a scientist checked the species and found that this was a new species and named it in honor of Dr. James Boehlke. This fish was collected by the author in Rio Araguaia, Brazil. Compare its color to the fish above.

This is the real *Thayeria obliqua* which, when it arrived in the United States from South America as an aquarium import, prompted a scientific investigation that resulted in a determination that the "new" fish is the old *Thayeria obliqua* and the "old" fish (above) is a new species. Photo by Dr. Herbert R. Axelrod.

One of the most popular of aquarium fishes is the black tetra, *Gymnocorymbus ternetzi*. A few years ago the author discovered that eastern European aquarists had a long-finned variety of the black tetra in their tanks, and this photograph shows the exact fish seen by the author in Czechoslovakia.

Dr. Karl Knaack, a Viennese dentist, took this photograph of a mature female black tetra, *Gymnocorymbus ternetzi*, with normal fins.

After breeding stock had been brought to the United States, a story about the long-finned black tetra appeared in *Tropical Fish Hobbyist* magazine where the writer, Joe Bellanca, gave them the nick-name G.T.O. which was derived from *Gymnocorymbus* (thus the "G") *ternetzi* (that's the "T"). . . and the "O" stands for the startling "OH". The fact that a popular automobile had a hard-selling campaign on for its GTO model at that time also aided in GTO becoming the standard name of this lovely fish. These are a pair of the first fish raised by the author in Florida, from which millions of fishes have subsequently been raised. Photo by the author.

Fishes of the genera *Copeina, Copella* and *Pyrrhulina* are all small, elongated characins found in South America. Typically they are found in very shallow, warm water, even water only a few inches deep. They have very interesting spawning habits and are usually very peaceful in the aquarium. The fish shown in the photograph to the right are *Copeina guttata*. Photo by Dr. Herbert R. Axelrod.

The most famous of the group is *Copeina arnoldi*, the splashing tetra. This fish lays its eggs out of the water on an overhanging leaf. The eggs are kept moist by the fish constantly splashing water against the leaf with its fins. The fish shown here is a male, as evidenced by the long dorsal fin and longer upper lobe of the tail. Photo by Hansen.

A very rare fish from South America is the spotted copeina, *Pyrrhulina spilota*. Photo by Dr. Herbert R. Axelrod.

Harald Schultz brought this fish to my laboratory directly from Brazil. I photographed it and we sent the specimens to Dr. Jacques Gery for identification. It turned out to be a new species and was named *Copella vilmae* to honor Harald Schultz' wife, Vilma Chiara Schultz. Harald died a few years later and no other *C. vilmae* ever were brought into the aquarium world. Photo by the author.

THE CYPRINIDS

Barbs, goldfish, koi and rasboras are all members of this very colorful and interesting group of fishes which are found in almost every aquarium or garden pool.

Whereas the characins, or tetras as they are more popularly (but less correctly) known, NEVER have barbels and MAY have an adipose fin, the cyprinids NEVER have an adipose fin and MAY have barbels. There are about as many different cyprinids as there are characins, roughly between 1,500 and 2,000 species. The cyprinids occur naturally in most of the world, except for the major island continents, such as Australia, New Zealand and Madagascar, and they are also missing from South America as far north as the Panama Canal, and the icy areas such as Alaska, Iceland and Greenland.

Cyprinids are usually fully scaled, although some man-made varieties (German carp, for example) may lack scales on part or all of the body; cyprinid scales are never found on the head.

Cyprinids may have barbels, some having as many as two pair of barbels, but never more. Unfortunately many ichthyologists violently disagree on how cyprinids should be separated into various genera, thus almost every book on cyprinids differs in nomenclature, especially as refers to the small aquarium fishes which aquarists refer to as barbs. Basically, the argument gets right to the heart of systematics and the problems are so important and the number of fishes involved so large, that it might be the work of a man's lifetime to sort out the situation.

A small peek into the problem might be interesting. Let's consider the barbs, those small aquarium fishes which are to be found in almost every aquarium store every place in the world. Some ichthyologists say they all belong to the genus *Barbus*, from which they derived their popular name barbs, since all are more or less anatomically related. However, should this position be accepted, it would

The four barbels shown on this fish will place it into the genus *Barbodes* according to Leonard P. Schultz. Photo by Dr. Herbert R. Axelrod.

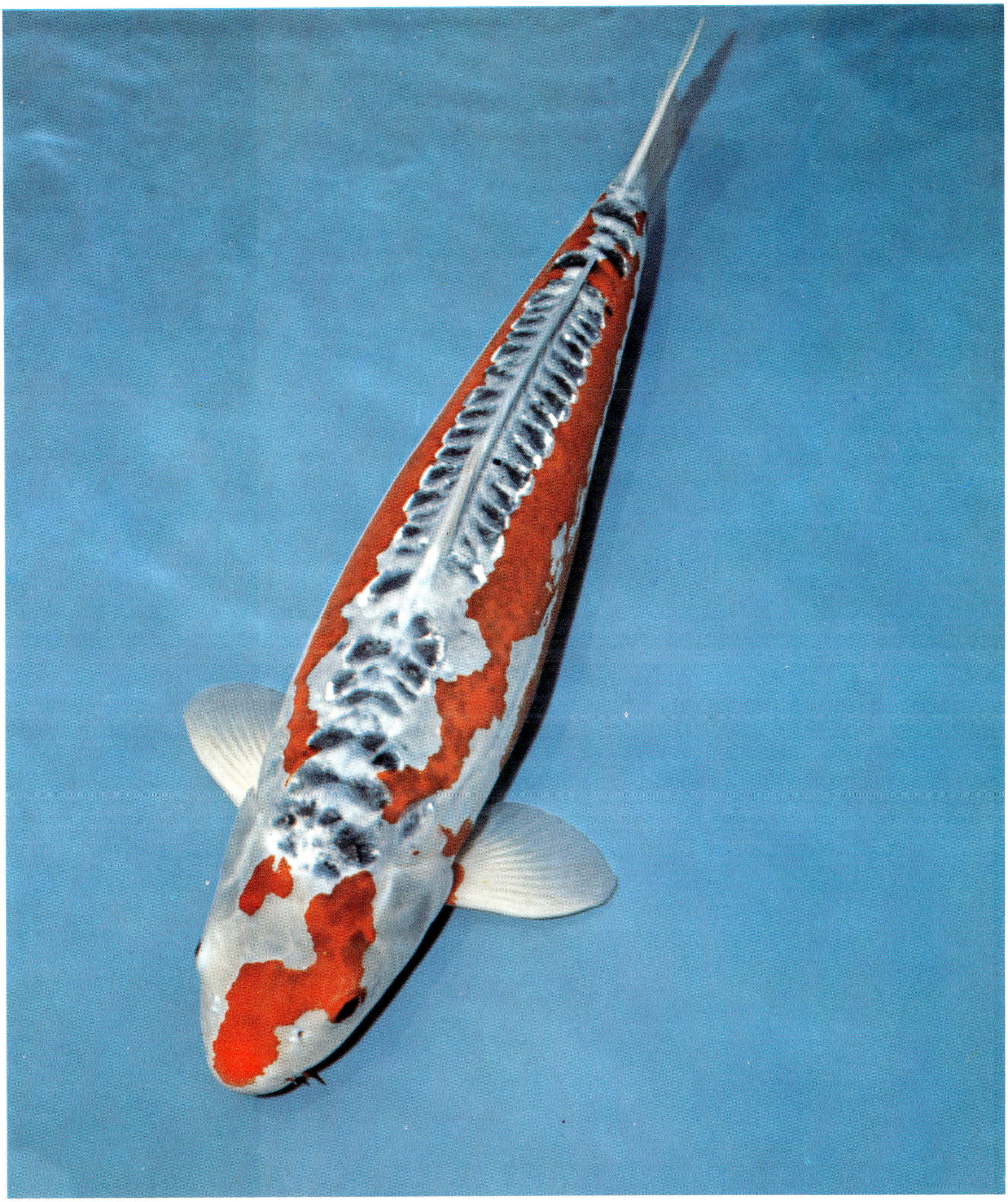

A shusui koi from Japan. This carp is about 28 inches long and is almost scaleless except for the line of scales along its back which identify it as the "German carp". In 1973 this fish was the champion shusui (a kind of Japanese carp) in the world!! From *Koi of the World* by Dr. Herbert R. Axelrod.

The goldfish comes in many varieties. One of the most weird is the bubble-eye, *Carassius auratus*. These are, of course, sports which have evolved through many generations of careful selective breeding; it is safe to suggest that there is almost no possibility that this sport will ever occur or survive in nature. Photo by Dr. Herbert R. Axelrod.

mean that fishes from such far away places as China, India and Ceylon, as well as the entire tropical part of southeast Asia, would be in the same genus as those barbs found throughout most of Africa. . . and they would all be in the same genus as the European barbel, *Barbus barbus*, the fish upon which Linnaeus in 1758 described the genus. *Barbus barbus* grows to about a yard in length and at one time was common from France to Hungary, including Britain! What is more amazing is that this is the only barb on the whole continent of Europe and is atypical of the rest of the barbs in that it grows very large and inhabits cold waters.

In order to get around the problem of calling these small tropical barbs *Barbus*, certain scientists have referred the problem to earlier workers (namely the famous ichthyologists Weber, de Beaufort, and Hugh M. Smith) who rejected the use of the genus *Barbus* in favor of the genus *Puntius*, and for many years this genus was the catch-all for the small, colorful tropical barbs.

Then along came Dr. Leonard P. Schultz, who was, at the time, curator of fishes at the U.S.N.M. (Smithsonian Institution). Dr. Schultz had his hand on the pulse of the aquarium trade and he appreciated the serious problems involved in the lack of a definitive work on the barbs, so he took the problem in hand and offered a very satisfactory solution. Of course he rejected the use of *Barbus* for anything except the cold-water giant from Europe; he said that *Puntius* might have been acceptable but it had too many fishes and the average hobbyist and scientist needed a more convenient division, so he suggested that we break up the barbs according to the numbers of barbels; those barbs with no barbels would be placed into the genus *Puntius*; those with one pair of barbels would be called *Capoeta*; and those with two pair would be classified under the genus *Barbodes*.

This very simple suggestion was not accepted by all systematists by any means. Those with books in print objected to this out-dating of their books; and those who previously supported *Puntius* could not find any better reason to support still another temporary classification. Yet in the aquarium trade the behavior of many fishes seems to classify them naturally along the lines that Schultz suggests; there seems to be some correlation between the behavior of a barb and the number of barbels it possesses. So I am supporting the Schultz classification until such time as a bright young ichthyologist devotes himself to the horrendous task of "working up" the barbs. The famous Schultz paper is presented in its basic entirety.

the generic names *Barbus* and *Puntius*

by Dr. Leonard P. Schultz
Curator of Fishes
U.S. National Museum

Weber and de Beaufort (*The fishes of the Indo-Australian Archipelago*, vol. 3, pp. 170-205, 1916) used the nominal genus *Puntius* Hamilton-Buchanan in place of *Barbus* Cuvier and Cloquet, for the cyprinids that are commonly called "barbs" by aquarists. However, the nomenclatorial and zoological facts concerning the use of *Puntius* and other generic names instead of *Barbus* for certain aquarium fishes has never been presented.

In the following discussion I shall develop the reasons, though complicated, why the genus *Barbus* cannot be applied correctly to any species of tropical aquarium fish. The "barbs" may be subdivided at least tentatively, into three genera as proposed by Bleeker almost a century ago. Gunther, Day and Boulenger were the authors who were mostly responsible for the misapplication of the nominal genus *Barbus* to a large group of African and Asiatic "barbs."

Cuvier and Cloquet (*Dictionnaire des sciences naturelles*, ed. 2, vol. 4, supp. p. 6, 1816) established the nominal genus *Barbus*, with *Barbus vulgaris* Cuvier and Cloquet proposed as a new name for *Cyprinus barbus* Linnaeus, a cyprinid fish from Europe.

The International Rules of Zoological Nomenclature in Article 30 I,d, state that "If a genus, without originally designated or indicated type (species) contains among its original spe-

The goldfish on the facing page has bubble eyes but no dorsal fin. This fish has a dorsal fin and a growth on its head. There are varieties with dorsal fins and those without, both varieties having the growth on the head. The Japanese call these orandas or lionheads (the lionhead translates from the Japanese "Oranda shishigeshira"). Photo by Dr. Herbert R. Axelrod.

There are many, many beautiful varieties of Japanese colored carp, or koi. Some, like these three "koshi no hisoku," are green with metallic coloration. The scales actually look like gold and are often thought to be artificially implanted pigment.

The hakushu koi is a hybrid produced from other koi varieties. Basically the fish is a platinum koi. Koi are, of course, carp and besides being ideal for the outdoor pools and ponds, they are good to eat! Photos from *Koi of the World*.

This kohaku koi is about 17 inches long and has an ideal color pattern on its back. The head patch almost completely covering the head yet completely separated from the next patch of red makes this such a valuable specimen. Depth of color and other characteristics make koi as valuable as $100,000 each for champions! Photo from *Koi of the World*.

cies one possessing the generic name as its specific or subspecific name, either as valid name or synonym, that species or subspecies becomes *ipso facto* type of the genus, (Type by absolute tautonymy)."

Since *Cyprinus barbus* Linnaeus was listed as one of the species under the nominal genus *Barbus, C. barbus* is the type species by tautonymy.

Bleeker (*Systema cyprinoideorum revisum*, Ned. Tijdschr. Dierk., vol. 1, p. 198, 1863; Atlas ichthyologique. . ., vol. 3, p. 26, 1863) was the first to designate the "Spec. type." of *Barbus* Cuvier and Cloquet and he selected *Barbus fluviatilis* Cuvier, which is a synonym of *Cyprinus barbus* Linnaeus. Thus it is well established that the type species of *Barbus* Cuvier and Cloquet 1816 is *Cyprinus barbus* Linnaeus.

Since the type species of *Barbus* is unquestionably *Barbus barbus* (Linnaeus), it is important to know by what characters this genus may be recognized. Some of these are as follows: Two pair of thick barbels, maxillary and rostral; pharyngeal teeth 4, 3, 2 + 2, 3, 4, all curved, hooked, and pointed; dorsal fin origin midway between snout tip and base of caudal fin; third dorsal ray, longest, bony, strong, and serrated along its posterior margin; gill membranes broadly joined to isthmus; scales small, about 35 to 38 rows in front of dorsal fin origin, 52 to 63 rows crossing lateral line; dorsal rays about iii, 8; anal iii, 5; pectoral about i, 16 or 17; pelvics i, 8 or 9; lateral line complete; vertebrae about 25 abdominal and 25 caudal totaling around 50.

The name *Barbus* has been used erroneously in ornithology in the generic sense by certain authors (Neave, *Nomenclator Zoologicus*, vol. 1, p. 393, 1939.) Cuvier, (*Tableau Elementaire de L'Histoire naturelle des animaux*, p. 234, 1798) used the name "barbus" for a group of birds. However it is the opinion of ornithologists that the name "barbus" was not used in the generic sense, but instead as a common name. Myers (*Stanford Ichthy. Bull.*, vol. 1, p. 170, 1940) states that "it is perfectly evident that 'barbus' of Cuvier 1798 is nothing more than the plural of Cuvier's vernacular appellation, 'barbus' for which birds Cuvier plainly uses the generic name *Bucco*." With that opinion I agree.

Puntius gelius is a very small barb which grows to only about 1½ inches in length. It comes from India but is so easy to breed that no one bothers to import any more wild ones, since tank-raised barbs are so much less expensive. Photo by G.J.M. Timmerman.

The checkerboard barb, *Capoeta oligolepis*, is another of the barbs which can be found in some aquarium books as either *Puntius* or *Barbus*, neither of which is correct. Photo by Rudolf Zukal.

Four barbels (two pairs) decorate the face of this cross between a male *Brachydanio rerio* and a female *Brachydanio albolineatus*. The hybrids were not very fertile and rather than inbreeding these hybrids, they are still produced by crossing the original species. Photo by the author.

Though the goldfish doesn't have any barbels, it can have a nasal ceres which decorates the face of this veiltailed goldfish. Photo by Dr. Herbert R. Axelrod.

This is the most widespread of the southeast Asian barbs ranging from the mainland of India to some of the offshore islands, including Sri Lanka (Ceylon). It has no barbels and has the scientific name of *Puntius vittatus* which was given it by Dr. Day in 1865. Photo by Dr. Herbert R. Axelrod.

From southeast India we have a barb which reaches almost 5 inches in length. The male has extended rays in his dorsal fin; these are absent in the female. Photo by Dr. Herbert R. Axelrod.

The nominal genus *Puntius* was established by Hamilton-Buchanan (*An account of the fishes found in the River Ganges and its branches*, p. 310, 1822.) Since *Cyprinus puntio* Hamilton-Buchanan was one of the species included under *Puntius*, by the rule of tautonymy it is the type species of the nominal genus *Puntius*, a parallel situation with that of *Barbus*.

Day (Proc. Zool. Soc. London, p. 100, 1870; *The Fishes of India*, vol. 2, p. 582, pl. 145, fig. 6, 1879) redescribed *Barbus puntio* (*Cyprinus puntio* Hamilton-Buchanan). Hora and Mukerji (Rec. Indian Mus., vol. 36, pt. 3, pp. 369-370, fig. 6, 1934) also recognize this species as *Barbus puntio*, which definitely gives it taxonomic status.

Therefore *Puntius puntio* (Hamilton-Buchanan) is unquestionably the type species of the nominal genus *Puntius* and the latter genus must be characterized by the anatomical features possessed by its type species.

Some of the anatomical characters of *Puntius puntio* are: no barbels; number of pharyngeal teeth not recorded; dorsal fin origin slightly closer to tip of snout than to base of caudal fin; the third dorsal "spine" bony, smooth and without serrations; gill membranes joined to isthmus; scales are large, about 11 or 12 in front of dorsal fin, and about 22 or 23 scale rows cross the lateral line; dorsal rays iii, 8; pectoral i, 14; pelvics i, 8; anal iii, 5; lateral line present, complete or incomplete.

Hora and Mukerji (l.c. p. 370) state that "*Barbus terio*" is closely allied to *puntio*, but the two species differ in certain body proportions, coloration and the extent of the lateral line.

Dr. H.M. Smith (*U.S. Nat. Mus. Bull.* 188, p. 165, 1945) called attention to the action of Bleeker (*Atlas Ichthyologique*, vol. 3, p. 27, 1863; *Ned. Tijdschr. Dierk.*, vol. 1, p. 200, 1863) who established 3 subgenera under the genus *Puntius*, with *Cyprinus* (*Puntius*) *sophore* Hamilton-Buchanan as type species of *Puntius*.

Bleeker's action for *Puntius* does not appear to be valid according to the International Rules of Zoological Nomenclature because (1) by tautonymy *Cyprinus puntio* Linnaeus is the type species and not *C. sophore*; (2) since sophore has 4 barbels it should not have been designated as the type species of *Puntius* which has no barbels according to Bleeker's diagnosis of his three subgenera, as follows:

Barbodes Bleeker, with 4 barbels (type species *Barbodes belinka* Bleeker.

Capoeta Cuvier and Valenciennes, with 2 barbels, type species *Capoeta amphibia* Cuvier and Valenciennes.

Puntius Hamilton-Buchanan, with no barbels.

The nominal genus *Capoeta* Cuvier and Valenciennes (*Histoire naturelle des poissons*, vol. 16, p. 278, 1842) was established with only three species assigned to it. Bleeker (l.c. p. 27) designated as type species *C. amphibia* Cuvier and Valenciennes which comes from Bombay. Bleekers designation appears to be correct nomenclatorially since Cuvier and Valenciennes do not list even as a synonym, *Barbus capoeta* Cuvier and Cloquet.

The nominal genus *Barbodes* was established by Bleeker (*Natuurk. Tijdschr. Ned. Ind.*, vol. 20, p. 431, 1859; Acta Soc. Sci. Ind. Ned., vol. 7, pp. 267, 275, 316, 1860) and Bleeker (l.c. p. 27, 1863) designated the type species of *Barbodes* as *B. belinka* Bleeker, which also appears to be correct nomenclatorially.

It is concluded therefore, that the genus *Barbus*, contains those cyprinid fishes of Europe with numerous (about 45 or more) small scales; numerous (about 50) vertebrae; and with 4 barbels, whereas the genus *Puntius* contains those cyprinid fishes of tropical Asia and Africa, with large scales of moderate number probably 17 to 33; vertebrae about 25 to 30 and no barbels.

This division leaves a large number of species formerly known as "barbs" that do not fit exactly into the genus *Puntius*. Among those with large scales (also about 17 to 33) and moderate numbers of vertebrae as in *Puntius puntio*, the following generic divisions would apply as set up by Bleeker, who dubbed them as subgenera.

Those species with four barbels should be assigned the generic name *Barbodes* Bleeker, whereas those with two barbels would belong to *Capoeta* Cuvier and Valenciennes. This arrangement may be artificial and somewhat tentative but it is the best that can

From the Indonesian Islands and Malaysia comes the zebra barb, *Barbodes fasciatus*. Photo by Dr. Karl Knaack.

Found in the same range as the above, *Barbodes schwanenfeldi* grows to more than a foot in length and has four barbels. This is a fairly young specimen. Photo by the author.

In 1897 the famous ichthyologist Dr. Weber described this barb as *Barbus viviparus*, now known as *Barbodes viviparus*. Despite it's specific name, it is not a livebearer! Photo by the author.

A lovely and very rare color in the goldfish is metallic chocolate brown. This fish was raised by a Chinese gentleman in Indonesia, where it was photographed by the author. The strain has never reached outside the Orient.

be done at the moment. Before more permanent conclusions can be reached extensive studies are required on the African and Asiatic "barbs" to untangle the mess resulting from earlier misunderstanding of the type species of *Barbus, Puntius, Capoeta, Barbodes* and other related nominal genera. These studies when completed may reallocate some of the species of "barbs" to genera other than those mentioned here.

Perhaps related to *P. conchonius*, this barb of the genus *Puntius* is a product of the Russian aquarist society which has produced several strains of barbs which have intense coloration. Here the barbs are spawning; the male is trying to entice the female into the dense vegetation.

How cyprinids breed

Cyprinids all lay eggs and almost always lay them in, on or under, dense clumps of vegetation, spraying them haphazardly or sticking them under leaves. Some eggs are very sticky and adhere to the plants, others are much less adhesive and fall wherever they are laid. Most cyprinids are difficult to sex when young and, except for some very special cases (*Capoeta hulstaerti*, for example), both sexes are colored alike except for a more intense coloration of the males of certain species during the breeding season. The females, as a rule, are almost always more plump than the males.

Cyprinids are very easy to spawn and some are merely thrown into large open pools in Florida where they spawn and live in relative peace and harmony with their offspring. For the home aquarist, however, some planning is necessary. It is a maxim in the fish breeding game to keep the sexes separate except for spawning. Cyprinids are far from the exception. The males should be isolated from the female, and both sexes should be heavily fed on live foods to prepare them for their reproductive roles. Most of the cyprinids are such gluttons that they can be counted on to eat almost anything. . . and everything. . . and I have often seen active barbs gobble up so much dry food so quickly, that their bellies almost burst as the food absorbed water and expanded inside the fish and they could hardly swim. This never happens with feedings of live food.

Finally the female follows the male; they wriggle against one another and spawn. Their eggs are tiny and numerous. It is not impossible to raise several thousand fry from one spawning of a 2-inch barb! Photos by Hans Joachim Richter.

How cyprinids spawn

Once the fishes have been conditioned for a few weeks on heavy live food feedings, the female will begin to bulge and the male will have heightened colors. At this time the breeding aquarium can be prepared. For most aquarium barbs, a 10-15 gallon aquarium will suffice. Since most barbs eat their eggs, I use lots of stones and marbles on the bottom of the tank and a dense bunch of spawning grass in the center of the tank. I usually introduce the female(s) into the tank the evening before I put in the males. Spawning usually takes place within hours of the opposite sex fishes being in contact. Spawns are usually large and the pairs should be removed as soon as spawning is complete. When is spawning complete? When the pair has stopped chasing through the spawning grass and they have stopped making bodily contact.

Cyprinids, by the way, have some common characteristics which are startlingly interesting. Many species, perhaps all species, spawn by lining up their bodies nose to nose, with their sides in contact; then the male drapes his caudal peduncle and tail over the female's back, using her raised dorsal fin as a pivot as he squeezes the eggs from her body.

The eggs hatch very quickly if the water is warm (about 80°F.) and the fry must have infusoria within 24 hours of their becoming free swimming or they will starve. Most cyprinid eggs are yellow or clear and are difficult to see without a strong light which highlights the eggs, especially if the light is shone through the glass bottom of the spawning tank.

The *Puntius* species continue spawning. Known as the Odessa barb in Russia, this obvious hybrid shows color dimorphism.

The male is red, as shown on the facing page; when he is just getting into breeding condition, he is silver with a reddish tinge. Photos by Hans Joachim Richter.

While spawning, the male will approach the female from the side and wrap his body over the top of hers, using her dorsal fin as a pivot.

When the female is finished spawning, she may hide buried in the dense vegetation to keep away from an insistent male who may kill her in his anxiety to spawn. Photos by Hans Joachim Richter.

There is obviously some connection between these barbs and those on the preceding pages, though a close comparison will indicate many differences in color. Photos by Hans Joachim Richter.

Another barb has come to us from Russia. This one has no name yet, though we might call it the scarlet barb, since the male is always scarlet when in top condition.

The black-spot barb was first described for science by Cuvier in 1844. The fish was originally described from India, but aquarium fish collectors also report it from Ceylon and other nearby areas. On the facing page are two adults spawning. Note the typical barb spawning behavior of the male wrapping his body about that of the female. The photo above shows what the young look like as compared to the adults on the facing page. The fish is known scientifically as *Puntius filamentosus*. Photos by Rudolf Zukal.

In 1871 Dr. Day described this new barb as *Barbus stoliczkanus* to honor a man named Stoliczka. By present-day standards of nomenclature the name of the fish has been changed to *Puntius stoliczkai*. The male has the red dorsal fin. Photo by Rudolf Zukal.

This barb, *Puntius stoliczkai*, comes from the Irrawaddy River in Burma. It probably occurs in other areas as well. The pair spawn in typical barb manner. Photo by Rudolf Zukal.

While collecting marine fishes on the island of Bandos near Male in the Maldive Islands, I discovered this small fish in the brackish water and in freshwater which we used for drinking purposes. It looked very much like *Capoeta chola*. Photo by the author.

Barbodes everetti, the clown barb, is found in Malaysia and Indonesia. It grows to 5 inches in length. In prior years this was a very popular fish, but lately it has fallen into disfavor because it is difficult to spawn.

Another of Sri Lanka's beauties is *Puntius cumingi*, which was originally described by Guenther in 1868. Photo by Klaus Paysan.

Could this be the real *Capoeta chola*? On the facing page was a photo of *Capoeta chola* from the Maldives (about 300 miles from Ceylon). The photo above shows the same (?) fish from Sri Lanka. Photo by Dr. Herbert R. Axelrod.

In 1973 the author visited with Rodney Jonklaas, the great Ceylonese naturalist. Jonklaas had just returned from southern India, bringing with him several "new" barbs. This fish was identified as *Puntius narayani*. Photo by Dr. Herbert R. Axelrod.

Puntius sachsi, or "Barbus schuberti" (a fantasy name which has no scientific value), in its tank-bred albino form. This fish is assumedly the albino form of the fish shown below. Photo by Dr. Herbert R. Axelrod.

Is this the real *Puntius sachsi*?? Is there really such a fish? Dr. Ahl described *Puntius sachsi* in 1923 as having come from Singapore. But no one has ever found the fish again and more fish are collected around Singapore than probably any other single area in the world! Photo by the author.

Barbodes fasciolatus, the African banded barb, ranges over a good part of western Africa. The fish is occasionally imported. The males always seem sickly and weak; the females are often more robust. Photo by Dr. Herbert R. Axelrod.

Capoeta semifasciolatus is supposed to range in China! It is so easily bred and China is so hard to reach for aquarium fishes that no one has verified that range to date! Millions of this fish are sold from Florida fish farms. Photo by G.J.M. Timmerman.

Most aquarium barbs come from India and Ceylon. *Puntius arulius*, shown here, was first described by Jerdon in 1849. He reported that it reached almost 5 inches in length. The fish is easily spawned, and the males often have longer dorsal rays. Photo by Rudolf Zukal.

Puntius callipterus is one of the oldest of the "common" barbs from Africa. It comes from near Lagos, Nigeria as well as from around ports in the Cameroons, so sailors brought the fish back to Europe as early as 1913. No one has ever reported spawning this species. Photo by Dr. Herbert R. Axelrod.

Dr. Karl Knaack sent us this photograph of a *Barbodes* species assumedly from Africa. No one has ever seen one before . . . or since!

Rodney Jonklaas says this is the true color of a breeding male *Puntius dorsalis*. He sent the author this photograph to prove it.

Puntius dorsalis is one of the common barbs in Sri Lanka, but it is rarely imported. Photo by Dr. Herbert R. Axelrod.

Barbodes hexazona is one of the tiger barb group. The male is the smaller, upper fish. Photo by the author.

Capoeta hulstaerti from Zaire (Congo) and a very difficult fish to keep alive. In its home range it is found in water which has a pH of about 4.0! Shown are two males; the females have no black in their fins. Photo by Dr. Herbert R. Axelrod.

Capoeta tetrazona originally came to aquarists from Sumatra and Borneo, but they are so very easy to breed that no one has bothered to import wild fish. Pieter Bleeker, the famous Dutch ichthyologist, described these fish in 1855, and almost every aquarist in the world has had them in his tanks at one time or another.

The tiger barb, *Capoeta tetrazona*, spawns typically, with the pair rushing into the thickets and rubbing their bodies frantically against each other as they spray fertilized eggs in all directions. Photos by Hans Joachim Richter.

As with most fishes which are inbred and cultivated by the millions, albinos were bound to show up. Here we have a pair of albino tiger barbs. Photo by Hugo Walters.

According to Hans Joachim Richter, who took this photo, this fish is the familiar *Puntius conchonius*. It differs considerably from the fish we know as the rosy barb.

Barbodes lateristriga, the spanner (monkey-wrench) barb. This is a young female. Photo by Dr. Herbert R. Axelrod.

Barbodes pentazona, another of the tiger barbs. This is a female. Photo by Rudolf Zukal.

A pair of cherry barbs, *Capoeta titteya*, in a spawning embrace. Photo by Rudolf Zukal.

The black ruby barb, *Puntius nigrofasciatus*. The male, lower fish, is not in breeding coloration. Comparatively drab when not in spawning coloration, the fish is very attractive in its spawning dress, as evidenced by the pair shown opposite. Photo by Rudolf Zukal.

A magnificent pair of *Puntius nigrofasciatus* in breeding color. The male gets a fiery red. As magnificent as this fish looks in a photograph, it is nothing compared with the real thing! I have seen them in Ceylon (now Sri Lanka) where they looked like they were covered with blood! They are fairly common in Ceylon. Photo by Hans Joachim Richter.

This photograph and the one below show *Rasbora daniconius* in typical spawning behavior. The pair push into thickets and the male wraps his body about that of the female as they lay their eggs in the thick vegetation. Photos by Rudolf Zukal.

Rasbora heteromorpha, the most frequently imported fish from southeast Asia, has been brought in by the millions every year. Yet, even with at least 100,000,000 collected mostly in their Malaysian range, they are still plentiful. The males are a bit more slender than the females. Photo by Hans Joachim Richter.

For many years the spawning of *Rasbora heteromorpha* was considered a big secret and an all but impossible feat. Then came the age of pH kits, and when aquarists found out they needed only an acid pH (below 6.0) and soft water plus a few *Cryptocoryne* plants, they were on their way.

The fish to the left is a plump female. Unless you select a good full female your chances of a successful spawning are almost nil.

The female is approached by a highly colored male *Rasbora heteromorpha*.

The female *Rasbora heteromorpha* deposits her eggs on the underside of the leaf of a *Cryptocoryne* plant while the male waits his turn to fertilize them.

The male *Rasbora heteromorpha* snuggles up next to the female and prepares to line himself up in a suitable spawning position.

He comes closer and closer to the female until. . .

He is perfectly lined up and then, in typical fashion, wraps his body about hers using the dorsal fin as a pivot point, fertilizing her eggs at the same time.

As they violently separate, some of the eggs are torn from the leaf; they will fall to the bottom to die or be eaten.

Photos in this series by Hans Joachim Richter.

There are various *Rasbora heteromorpha*-like species in southeast Asia. Some ichthyologists call this a separate species because it is smaller and because the black triangle is less intense in its blackness and has a smaller extension of black. In any case it is *Rasbora heteromorpha espei*.

The photo above and the two photos on the facing page show *Rasbora heteromorpha espei* spawning. The importance of these photos is that the pair have selected a *Cryptocoryne* leaf similar to those found in their native habitat in preference to other heavy-leafed plants from South America. Notice the wrapping of the male's body about the female's, using her dorsal fin as a pivot. Photos in this series by Rudolf Zukal.

The black triangle and the black mark over the anal fin base are highly variable in size. This specimen has a dot on the caudal peduncle, the specimen below has no dot.

These fish laid a few eggs on the top of the *Cryptocoryne* leaf before they started spawning upside down under the leaf. This is the true *Rasbora heteromorpha*. Notice the shape of the black triangle. Photo by Rudolf Zukal.

These two photographs show still another kind of *Rasbora heteromorpha* in which the point of the black triangle goes right into the tail and which has almost no black marking on the base of the anal fin. Photos by Hans Joachim Richter.

Rasbora elegans comes from Malaysia and the Sunda Islands. They are a very peaceful species and make a good addition to the home aquarium. Photo by the author.

Rasbora einthoveni has a fairly widespread distribution from Singapore to Thailand, with island locations in between. It is a lovely, peaceful species and is highly recommended for the community aquarium. Photo by the author.

Rasbora borapetensis is found only in Thailand and, as you can see from the photograph, the female is quite robust while the male looks almost sickly. This is normal, however. Photo by the author.

Rasbora maculata, one of the tiny *Rasbora* species. Photo by Klaus Paysan.

Rasbora kalochroma. Photo by the author.

Rasbora somphongsi, perhaps the most tiny of the *Rasbora* species, was named to honor Somphongs Lekaree, the first and largest exporter of aquarium fishes from Thailand. Somphongs died in 1972 after making millions in the fish exporting business. The lower fish is a female and spawned shortly after this photo was taken. Photo by the author.

Rasbora dusonensis. Photo by G.J.M. Timmerman.

Rasbora urophthalmus. The male is the upper fish and the more slender of the pair. Photo by Dr. Stanislav Frank.

The scissorstail *Rasbora*, the most easily spawned in the genus, is scientifically known as *Rasbora trilineata*. The upper fish is the female. She is much more robust than the male. Photo by Rudolf Zukal.

Upper left: *Rasbora vaterifloris* photographed by the author in Ceylon. The fish become a beautiful deep violet when in spawning condition. Top right: *Rasbora caudimaculata*. Photo by the author. Center: *Rasbora pauciperforata*. Photo by Dr. Stanislav Frank. Below: *Rasbora dorsiocellata*. Photo by Klaus Paysan.

The zebra danio, *Brachydanio rerio*, comes from the eastern side of India and was first discovered and described by Hamilton-Buchanan in 1822! It is a very popular aquarium fish raised by the millions every year by every commerical fish breeding operation that deals with aquarium fishes. Zebras lay non-adhesive eggs and are very prolific. Photo by Hans Joachim Richter of a male.

Danio devario was described by Hamilton-Buchanan at the same time he described *Brachydanio rerio* in 1822. This fish is also found in India. Photo by Klaus Paysan.

Danio malabaricus is found in Sri Lanka and western India. It is bred in large quantities, easily, and no importations of wild stock are required. Photo by Rudolf Zukal.

This is one of the aquarium world's mysteries. Suddenly some East German aquarists proclaimed they had discovered a new fish "from somewhere in China." They even had a nice name for it, *Brachydanio frankei*. No one has ever found this fish in nature, so we take the scientific name with a grain of salt. A fish has to exist in nature for it to be a new species; fish which are developed as hybrids or sports cannot be given new scientific names. Photo by Dr. Herbert R. Axelrod.

Dr. Stanislav Frank of Prague, Czechoslovakia sent me photographs of this *Brachydanio nigrofasciatus* which Dr. Day described in 1869 as having come from Burma, where it is very widely distributed, occurring almost everywhere.

The normal *Brachydanio rerio*, the zebra fish. Photo by Dr. Stanislav Frank.

By crossing the top two fish, that is, by crossing a female *Brachydanio rerio* with a male *Brachydanio nigrofasciatus*, you end up with a hybrid that looks like this one. Photo by Dr. Stanislav Frank.

Brachydanio kerri was described by Hugh M. Smith in 1931 as a new species he discovered in Koh Yao Yai, an island off the coast of Thailand. Compare this species carefully with *B. albolineatus* (below) and you might not be able to find any significant differences. Photo by Dr. Stanislav Frank.

Brachydanio albolineatus was first described by Blyth in 1860 as ranging in India and Sumatra. Undoubtedly it exists in other areas as well and might very well be the same fish which Hugh M. Smith described in 1931 as having a range in some islands off the coast of Thailand. Photo by the author of a heavy female hovering over a slender male.

Esomus danricus was described by Hamilton-Buchanan in 1822 as having come from India, Sri Lanka, Thailand and Malaysia. It has two pairs of barbels; the maxillary barbels (on the upper jaw) are very long and may be about half as long as the fish, while the snout barbels are short and fleshy. The male is slender. Photo by Gene Wolfsheimer.

The Dutch ichthyologist Bleeker described *Balantiocheilus melanopterus* in 1850 from Indonesia and Thailand. It grows to about 14 inches in length. This specimen was photographed in the Berlin Aquarium in Berlin, Germany where Werner Schroeder has one of the best fish exhibits in the world. Photo by Dr. Herbert R. Axelrod.

At the same time that he described the above species, Bleeker also described *Epalzeorhynchus kallopterus*, which is also found in Indonesia (Borneo and Sumatra). It stays below 6 inches in length and spends most of its time resting on its pectoral fins on the bottom of the tank. It has two pairs of barbels. Photo by the author.

Epalzeorhynchus kallopterus resting on a leaf in a tank in the Berlin Aquarium. The special fringed processes on the mouth enable this fish to do special things. . . the least of which is to eat planarian worms from the bottom sand!! It also grazes on algae, which makes it a very desirable creature for the home aquarium. Photo by H. Hansen.

Rudolf Zukal, Czechoslovakia's outstanding fish photographer, caught this *Labeo bicolor* with its barbels outstretched and its fins wide open. The author, in the early 1960's, discovered the breeding grounds of *Labeo bicolor* in Thailand with Somphongs Lekaree. We experimented in shipping them back at a size of about half an inch long, with about 2,000 in two gallons of water and were thus able to reduce their price to aquarists substantially. They grow very rapidly.

Thailand has several *Labeo* species, and this one, *Labeo frenatus*, has been around the literature only since 1934, when Fowler described it from specimens found in Chingmai. It closely resembles an African *Labeo* from the Nile, *Labeo forskali*. What is most interesting is that the Nile *Labeo* grows to 14 inches while the Thai *Labeo* barely reaches 4 inches in total length. Photos by Rudolf Zukal.

The fish shown in the photograph above is *Labeo cylindricus* from Africa. The fish to the left is an unidentified species of *Labeo* which was collected and photographed by Dr. Jacques Gery. The fish shown below is *Labeo altivelis*. *Labeo altivelis*, *Labeo cylindricus* and *Labeo congoro*, shown on the facing page, were all collected and photographed by Dr. Eugene Balon and are from his book *Fishes of Lake Kariba, Africa*.

Labeo congoro is a magnificent black *Labeo* with a huge dorsal fin. It would make a magnificent aquarium fish, but no one is exporting fishes from Zambia's Lake Kariba. Photo by Dr. Eugene Balon.

The black shark, *Morulius chrysophekadion*, comes from Thailand and the Greater Sunda Islands. It was first described by Bleeker in 1849. It is not a shark at all, but the name sticks in aquarists' circles based upon the appearance of the dorsal fin. While it is very popular because it is easily captured and shipped along with other Thai fishes, I much prefer the *Labeo congoro* for beauty. Photo by Klaus Paysan.

Many *Labeo* species are food fishes, and some grow very large. *Labeo lunatus*, shown above, grows fairly large and is an important food fish from Lake Kariba, Zambia. Note the lip shape! Photo from Dr. Eugene Balon's book *Fishes of Lake Kariba, Africa.*

Labeo lunatus is another of the beautiful black *Labeo* species from Lake Kariba. Photo by Dr. Eugene Balon.

It is often very difficult to appreciate the beauty and color of the White Cloud Mountain fish from China, but Aaron Norman captured this fish in all its splendor. Usually the white cloud, *Tanichthys albonubes*, is constantly moving, making observation very difficult.

A pair of white clouds spawning. Note the way the male wraps his body about that of the female, using her dorsal fin as a pivot. This spawning characteristic seems to be limited to the family Cyprinidae. Photo by Rudolf Zukal.

Long-finned white clouds have appeared in Canada and Czechoslovakia. Photo of a pair of long-finned white clouds called "meteor minnows" with the female the upper, stouter fish. Photo by Dr. Herbert R. Axelrod.

This is the bed of a typical clear, cool stream in southeast Asia. This stream happens to be in Burma, but you can see how the many rocks and the swift current would favor the development and evolution of fishes which use their mouths as holdfast organs as well as for eating algae. Photo by Peter Tsang.

The photo to the left is actually in the same stream in Burma as that above, but it shows how the Burmese catch fish. They slowly trickle a stream of water containing rice juices into the stream to attract fishes which hide under the rocks, then with a very fast scooping motion they lift the rocks and net the fish hiding under them. They manage to collect lots of loaches and "sharks" that way. Photo by Peter Tsang. The photo below shows another type of Burmese habitat where gouramis, puffers and *Rasbora* range. Photo by the author.

The coolie (sometimes spelled kuhli) loach, *Acanthophthalmus semicinctus*. Photo by Dr. Herbert R. Axelrod.

Coolie loaches get their name from the scientific name of the fish *Acanthophthalmus kuhli*. Photo by Arend van den Nieuwenhuizen.

Acanthophthalmus shelfordi is another of the coolie loaches. These fish only get to about 4 inches in length and make excellent scavengers in the home aquarium, though you rarely can find them. Photo by the author.

All of the coolie loaches on this page are *Acanthophthalmus shelfordi*, and if you want to be very technical about it, all of the coolie loaches shown in this book are probably the same species. The main difference between these fishes is their color pattern. If the markings are basically irregular, then the fish is called *A. shelfordi*, which ranges in Borneo and has a total of 7 spines and rays (usually 2 spines and 5 rays) in its dorsal fin. The fish is relatively slender. Photos by Dr. Herbert R. Axelrod.

These two loaches are known as *Acanthophthalmus semicinctus*. They come from Singapore, but the true range of *A. semicinctus* is the East Indies. These fish are thicker than the *A. shelfordi* on the facing page, and they have a total of 8 to 9 spines and rays in their dorsal fin. Photos by Dr. Herbert R. Axelrod.

Acanthophthalmus myersi is essentially the same as *A. semicinctus* except for the markings and its thickness. It has a total of 10 spines and rays (usually 2 spines and 8 rays) in its dorsal fin. This fish comes from Thailand. Photo by Dr. Herbert R. Axelrod.

Three species (?) of *Acanthophthalmus*: from front to back, a new species which has no bars and has no scientific name at the moment; a weirdly marked fish with a black tail and a ring about the caudal peduncle; and *A. kuhlii*. Photo by Vojtec Elek.

Acanthophthalmus javanicus imported by Jack Roberts of Roberts Fish Farm in Miami, Florida.

A close-up of the faces of the two weirdly marked *Acanthophthalmus* (see lower photo page 155) which were photographed by Vojtec Elek in Prague, Czechoslovakia. There is speculation that these fish were collected in North Vietnam.

Botia modesta was described by Bleeker in 1865. It ranges over most of the tropical areas in the monsoon belt of southeast Asia from Malaysia through Vietnam and Thailand. Photo by Dr. Herbert R. Axelrod.

Burkhard Kahl, the great German aquarist and fish photographer, supplied the author with photographs of some of his loaches in superb condition. The two loaches above are *Botia sidthimunki*, which Dr. Klausewitz described, from Thailand. Assumedly this shows a pair, though sex differences in loaches are unknown. The fish on the left is the most sought after *Botia macracantha* from Indonesia, while the lower fish is *Botia beauforti* from Thailand.

A very pretty fish is the Pakistani loach, *Botia lohachata*, which was described by Chaudhuri in 1912. It reaches barely 4 inches in length and is not too often seen in aquariums because of the infrequency with which Pakistani fishes are exported. Photo by Dr. Herbert R. Axelrod.

Widely distributed throughout Thailand is *Botia horae*, which was first described by Hugh M. Smith in 1931. Its coloration with the oblique band is very similar to a *Corydoras* which is similarly marked. Photo by the author.

The clown loach, *Botia macracantha*, is the most widely sought after loach. Thus far no one has succeeded in regularly spawning any of the loaches on a commercial scale, but success will come soon as the techniques of using hormones in small fishes is perfected. Photo by Dr. Herbert R. Axelrod.

A close-up of the face of *Botia macracantha* shows the four pairs of barbels fairly clearly. Most *Botia* poke about the bottom of their habitat, and the barbels serve for the location of food as well as for tactile purposes. Note the inferior (underslung) mouth. The indentation under the eye is for the orbital spine which may project from under the eye to discourage another fish from attacking. Photo by the author.

Botia beauforti. Photo by Gene Wolfsheimer.

This series of four photographs shows the color development in what is probably a *Botia lohachata* relative from India, known as *B. dario*. Our friend Rodney Jonklaas found these in an Indian pet shop and photographed the series for us. It was so humid there that the film actually developed a fungus, thus the mottling on the photographs.

A young specimen of *Botia horae* which still shows the stripes. *Botia modesta* juveniles are similarly striped. Photo by Klaus Paysan.

Botia sidthimunki. This may be the first loach to be spawned, since there are always thin and robust specimens which suggest sex differences. Photo by the author.

THE ANABANTOIDS

The author collecting in Indonesia, where the water is so heavily laden with algae that on sunless days the carbon dioxide actually bubbles! A huge giant gourami was netted.

In downtown Djakarta there are areas where scores of tropical fish shops, open air affairs, offer fishes for sale in unaerated tanks and jars. Gouramis are a favorite, since they get along so well without aeration. Photo by the author.

ANABANTOIDS

A large group of fishes found in southeast Asia, including the Philippines, and in almost all of Africa south of the desert, require atmospheric air in order to breathe. Not all of the fishes in this range require air from the atmosphere, and not all fishes which require air are anabantoids (such as the *Corydoras* catfishes of South America, for example). What separates the anabantoids is the labyrinth chamber, a special organ composed of lamellae which are covered over with a special blood-soaked thin skin, enabling the fish to utilize atmospheric air. Lamellae are a series of thin plates which look very much like the underside of a mushroom cap. Engineers copied this structure for cooling and dispersing heat, as in the fins on a car radiator.

It seems that through the process of evolution certain fishes had to live in water which contained so much decaying matter, or was so algae-rich, that the oxygen available in the water was below that which was required by the fish. So that now all anabantoids MUST have atmospheric air or they will perish. I learned this lesson on my first collecting trip to Thailand. I put a trap in the water one night, coming back the next morning to see what I had collected. Several paradisefish and some bettas were in the trap. . . all dead! They had suffocated since they could not get out of the trap and up to the surface to breathe!

While the possession of a labyrinth organ is one of the major bases for the scientific classification of the several families of fishes in the suborder Anabantoidei, our aquarium anabantoids have certain other common characteristics as well.

For the most part all of those from Asia build a bubblenest in order to keep their eggs together in a nest. The bubblenest is usually constructed by the male who, after he has completed the nest, entices a female under it to spawn. Some nests are very complex and large (*Betta, Colisa, Trichogaster*)

A typical pond in Indonesia where gouramis, *Rasbora* species and other fishes are to be found. Air breathing is a necessity for many fishes because they require more oxygen than the water carries. This pond yielded blue gouramis, *Trichogaster trichopterus*. Photo by Dr. Herbert R. Axelrod.

Anabas testudineus, shown here in a xanthistic color form, is a highly undesirable aquarium fish. It ranges widely over southeast Asia, even to the Philippines, and I even collected some from a ditch near Palmetto, Florida! They had escaped from a fish farm and had established themselves! This fish has a very bad reputation for climbing trees and chasing dogs!! How deserved is this reputation is unknown, but it is known as the climbing perch. . . though it's not a perch!

while some are hardly recognizable (*Helostoma*). Some nests are even built underwater by some of the smaller anabantoids.

The male blows bubbles with the aid of a mucus secretion from his mouth. Once he has attracted a female and spawned with her by squeezing her body with his own as he forms a tight "U" shape, she seems to be paralyzed for a few seconds, giving the male time to gather the eggs, or in the case of species that have floating eggs, giving the eggs a chance to float up into the nest. Once the female "awakens" she usually eats any of the eggs that she finds outside the nest.

When spawning is complete, the male guards the nest, capturing any eggs or (later) any newly hatched young that escape from the nest and blowing them back into the nest.

A few species of anabantoids are even mouthbrooders (some species of *Betta*). Generally speaking, the anabantoids from southeast Asia have complex nests while those from Africa have almost non-existent nests. I have observed *Ctenopoma* spawning and was never able to detect a nest, but in

Belontia signata, the combtail paradisefish, is found in Ceylon where it looks nothing like our photograph. The usual color of the fish is red when the fish is in breeding color. They are not friendly fishes and are not recommended for the home aquarium unless you are an anabantoid specialist. Photo by Dr. Stanislav Frank.

E. Roloff, the very well known fish expert from Karlsruhe, Germany, collected this beautiful Siamese fighting fish which doesn't fight, so he dubbed it the 'peaceful betta.' Dr. Ladiges described this as a new species and named it *Betta smaragdina*. Photo by E. Roloff.

From Malaysia comes this lovely *Betta bellica*. The fish shown is a male; while it is not the most colorful fish in the world, the wild form of this species is more colorful at times than the wild form of *Betta splendens*. Photo by the author.

In 1935 Dr. George Myers described a new species of fighting fish from Java and Sumatra as *Betta brederi* to honor Dr. Breder of the American Museum of Natural History. We are indebted to Mr. E. Roloff for this photograph of a male with a mouthful of eggs.

Siamese fighting fish, *Betta splendens*, have been bred in many color varieties. The ideal colors are those which have only one color in them. This lavender blue fish is the most difficult solid color to breed. Photo by Dr. Karl Knaack, Vienna.

several magazine articles observers of *Ctenopoma congicum* claim that a nest is built. It is very possible that fishes spawn differently under different circumstances, as I have seen some *Betta splendens* build huge nests, while others seem to be happy with just a few bubbles.

Another rather common characteristic of anabantoids is that they usually (except for the mouthbrooders) have a huge spawn. The kissing gourami, *Helostoma*, may have thousands of eggs, as do the fishes of the genus *Trichogaster* and *Colisa*. Thus, if you wish to spawn these fishes you must be prepared for a large brood. Certainly it is unthinkable to attempt to spawn and raise the family of any anabantoid in less than a 10-gallon tank. . . and a 50-gallon tank might even be better! It is not merely a matter of crowding, because once the fish reach a certain size their labyrinth organs develop and they can live on atmospheric air; it is also a matter of fighting over food and chomping on the fins of their too-close-by brethren.

The ballet of spawning anabantoids is so beautiful and so easy to precipitate that anyone who has an aquarium and doesn't prepare a pair of Siamese fighting fish, *Betta splendens*, for spawning is missing one of the greatest thrills our hobby has to offer.

Male Siamese fighting fish have the longer fins and they are the ones who have the responsibility of building the bubble nests! Photo by Rudolf Zukal.

This is a male chocolate Siamese fighting fish, *Betta splendens*. This is the very rarest of complete colors, though everyone is striving for a perfect black. Photo by Dr. Herbert R. Axelrod.

Dr. Gene Lucas, recognized as one of the world's outstanding authorities on Siamese fighting fish since he wrote his ph.D. thesis on them, has given us this photo of a very rare white betta.

The length of finnage and the intensity of color makes this beautiful male *Betta splendens* a champion fish. Photo by Hans Joachim Richter.

A male *Colisa fasciata,* also called the giant gourami for some reason, rarely reaches five inches in length. This fish is spitting some eggs into his bubblenest. Photo by Hans Joachim Richter.

A pair of *Colisa fasciata* circle each other under a floating leaf which has a few rudimentary bubbles under it to signal the female where she is to spawn. The male bends his body into a U-shape into which the female snuggles to have the eggs squeezed from her. Photo by Hans Joachim Richter.

As soon as the female has fit into the male's bent body, he squeezes her and both fish fall to the bottom of the tank in an ecstasy which results in the female's remaining paralyzed for a few seconds as the eggs float up to the surface, hopefully into the nest. Compare this species to *Colisa labiosa*. I haven't been able to differentiate between them. Photo by Hans Joachim Richter.

Colisa lalia, the dwarf gourami, is found in Assam and Bengal in India, where they are quite common. They are so easy to breed that no new imports of any quantity have been reported in 30 years. This male was photographed by Dr. Karl Knaack.

Colisa labiosa about to embrace under a nest formed by floating plants. Photo by Rudolf Zukal.

A male *Colisa labiosa* in breeding color. Compare this fish to *Colisa fasciata*. Photo by Hansen.

Colisa chuna, the honey gourami, spawning under his bubblenest amidst suspended eggs. In the background, hardly visible, is the female. These are very small gouramis and extremely delicate and shy. In breeding color they are, as you can see, magnificently shaded. Photo by Hans Joachim Richter.

There are supposed to be two species of kissing gourami, the pink one, *Helostoma temmincki,* and the green one, known as *Helostoma rudolfi*. The authenticity of these names has to be checked. The photo above shows a "pair" of white kissers doing just that. Photo by D. Terver, Nancy Aquarium, Nancy, France.

A green kisser and a white kisser enjoying a meal of freeze-dried tubifex worms from a feeding bell. Photo by David Chen.

A white kisser, *Helostoma temmincki*, showing a special pigmentation which some people feel is a disease. It does not, however, seem to affect the health or activity of the fish. Photo by Hans Joachim Richter.

This photograph was the first ever made showing the way chocolate gouramis spawn! The pair embrace in typical gourami style and the huge, heavy eggs merely fall out of them onto the ground where they are then picked up in the mouth of the female to be incubated. Photo by Hans Joachim Richter.

This *Osphronemus goramy* is the one I caught in the pond illustrated on page 162. This one weighs about 5 pounds; I took its photo out of water. The photo to the right below is the same species at 4 inches in length.

A male chocolate gourami, *Sphaerichthys osphromenoides*, from Malaysia. This fish shows the typical fright or night color pattern. Photo by Hans Joachim Richter.

From Thailand comes the sleek moonlight gourami, *Trichogaster microlepis*. This fish grows to about six inches and is very peaceful and quiet. It is highly recommended for the community tank. Photo by the author.

Another very beautiful and peaceful gourami is the pearl gourami, *Trichogaster leeri*. These fish are about to spawn under their meager bubblenest. Photo by Hans Joachim Richter.

The blue gourami, *Trichogaster trichopterus*, is probably represented in different areas by separate color varieties or subspecies. The fish shown upper left is the typical blue gourami which is also known as the three-spot blue gourami. This is, more or less, the color pattern of the normal wild fish. The photo upper right is the first color variety which completely lost the spots and which featured the black mottled coloration. This eventually developed into the Cosby gourami. Cosby was a breeder who is credited with having first developed this color variety. Photos by the author.

East German aquarists developed a beautiful golden variety of the "blue" gourami, *Trichogaster trichopterus*, which became an instant success as soon as they hit the aquarium market. Photo by Hans Joachim Richter.

The beautiful golden gourami in a spawning embrace beneath the bubblenest. As usual, the male forms a "U" with his body, enticing the female into the embrace. This variety is very prolific, with thousands of eggs laid at each spawning. Photo by Hans Joachim Richter.

A beautiful male *Trichopsis schalleri*. The subspecies or race called *schalleri* is probably derived from *Trichopsis vittatus*. Here we see the male tending the nest of eggs which was placed under this overhanging leaf. Photo by Hans Joachim Richter.

The snakeskin gourami, *Trichogaster pectoralis* from Malaysia and Thailand. It grows a bit large for the aquarium, about 8 inches, and is not a delicate fish at all. Its lack of color has not made it one of aquarists' favorites. Photo by the author.

Macropodus cupanus dayi is a beautiful little paradisefish which has never become popular because it is too difficult for the mass producers of aquarium fishes to breed. This is a nice male. Photo by Hans Joachim Richter.

Macropodus opercularis is a relatively cold water species from Taiwan, Korea and China. It is very pugnacious and hardy and is not recommended for the community tank. The fish shown here is a male. Photo by the author.

Bred by the millions in Florida fish farms during the 1940-1970 period, it was most likely that the paradisefish would produce an albino from which constant inbreeding of the progeny would produce a strain of albinos. Albino paradise, sometimes referred to in the trade as white paradise, are very popular because they seem to be less pugnacious than their normally colored brethren. Photo by the author.

Rudolf Zukal took this magnificent photograph of a male black paradise which, although currently classified as *Macropodus opercularis*, is undoubtedly a different species.

Another color variety of the paradisefish is the one from the Ryukyu Islands. This is called the red paradisefish in the trade. Here we see a male in all his magnificent coloration as he prepares his bubblenest for spawning. Photo by Hans Joachim Richter.

The croaking gourami, *Trichopsis pumilus*, is well known to aquarist-soldiers who were in Saigon, Vietnam during the war as this is their range! It is very small, not reaching 1½ inches in length. The male shown here is in spawning coloration. Photo by Hans Joachim Richter.

One of Hans Joachim Richter's most startling photographs is this spawning embrace of a pair of croaking gouramis, *Trichopsis pumilus*.

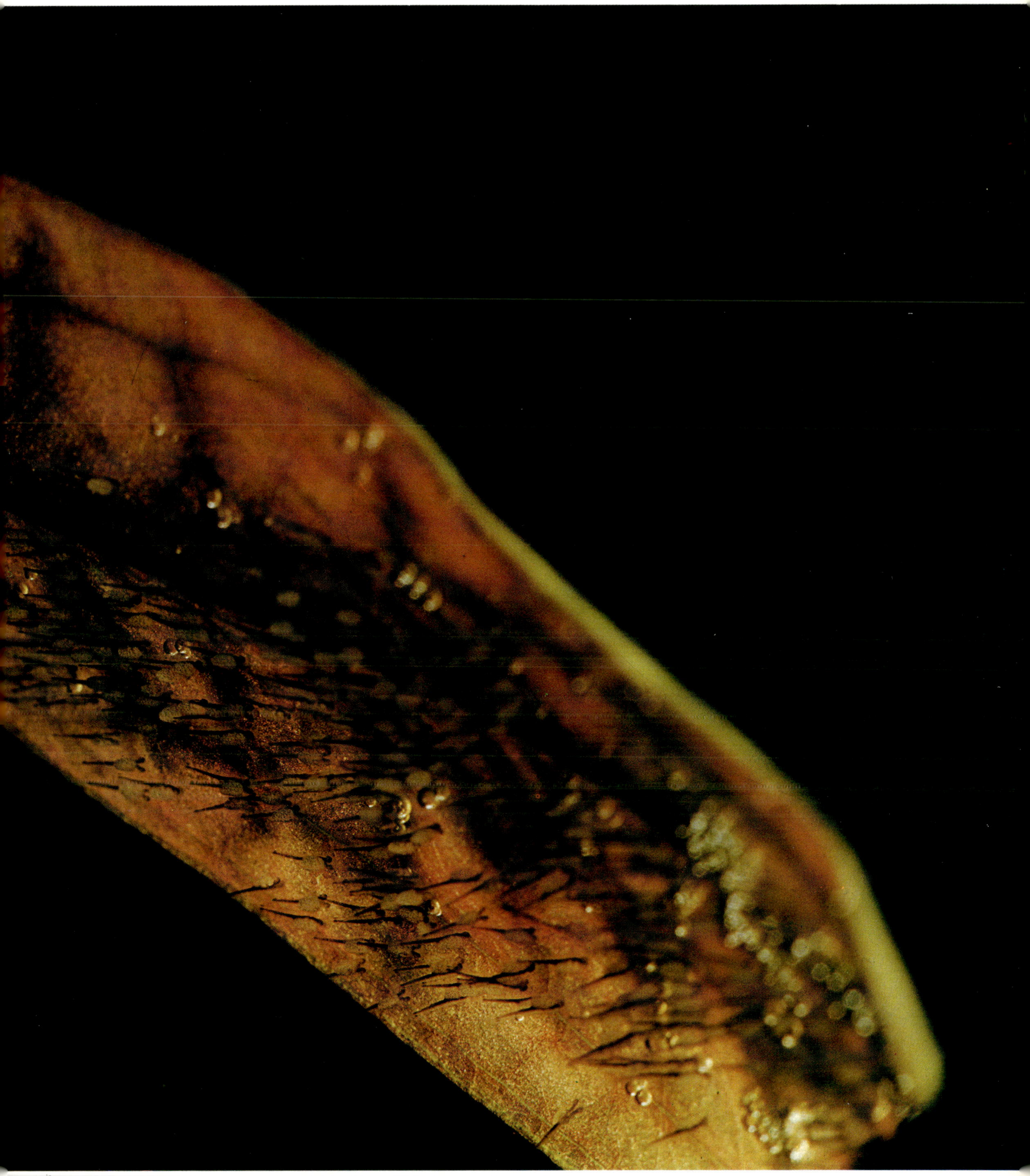

Trichopsis vittatus schalleri nest, the same one shown on the top of page 182, showing the eggs just hatched. Photo by Hans Joachim Richter.

Ctenopoma maculatus is from somewhere in Africa. It is very rare and until Hans Joachim Richter received a few fish, no one knew anything about their care or breeding. On the facing page, the upper fish is the female and the lower fish is the male. IN the photo above they get to know each other immediately prior to spawning. Photos by Hans Joachim Richter.

The pair circle each other slowly until they finally jockey into the usual nuptial embrace peculiar to most anabantids.

After the female has released the eggs, the lighter than water eggs float gently in all directions. If no other fishes eat them, they will hatch into baby *Ctenopoma maculatus*. Photos by Hans Joachim Richter.

On page 182 (top photograph) we showed the *schalleri* variety of *Trichopsis vittatus*. The fish shown here is the other variety. This is a male displaying before another male in a typically combative position. Photo by Hans Joachim Richter.

Ctenopoma nanum was described by Guenther in 1896 ranging from the Cameroons to Zaire. Not too much is known about this fish, though the literature suggests they spawn in typical anabantid fashion. This is the photograph of a young female. Photo by the author.

From the Stanley Pool area of Zaire comes this very well known anabantid, *Ctenopoma fasciolatum*. The fish was first described by Boulenger in 1899. Photo by Kremser.

From Chiloanga and Ubangi in Zaire, comes *Ctenopoma congicum*. It was first described by Boulenger in 1887 and reportedly grows to 3½ inches. I photographed this fish in Pierre Brichard's compound in Kinshasa in 1969. The long fins indicate this to be a male.

Ctenopoma nigropannosum was described by Reichenow in 1875 with a wide range between the Congo and Niger Rivers. I photographed this specimen in Brichard's compound at the same time as I photographed *congicum* above. This is a female.

Boulenger in 1912 described *Ctenopoma ansorgei* from Chiloanga and tropical west Africa. It barely reaches three inches and even though this specimen looks highly colored, the male is even more so! Photo by Aaron Norman.

Ctenopoma kingsleyae was described by Guenther in 1896 and is widely distributed all over the Congo River system. It is not at all colorful, but it is very available. Photo by the author.

Pellegrin described this fish in 1899 as *Ctenopoma acutirostre*. It ranges along the Congo River and has been called the leopard *Ctenopoma*. None of these fish are beyond eating anything small enough to swallow in one gulp and with their rather large mouth it is small wonder the cardinal tetra, *Cheirodon axelrodi*, is just peeking from behind the stone! Photo by the author.

Ctenopoma oxyrhynchus from the Congo River. These are fairly young fish, about 3½ inches long, sexually indistinguishable at this age. The white spots are the common disease caused by the parasite *Ichthyophthirius*. Photo by the author.

THE CICHLIDS

THE CICHLIDS

The sunfishes and basses, with which most anglers are familiar, are "replaced" in Africa, South and Central America, and by one genus in Southeast Asia, by the family Cichlidae. The cichlids are very similar to sunfishes in many ways, including their general shape, but they do have some very important diagnostic differences. One easily observed difference is the number of nostrils to be found on the side of the head. Cichlids have but one nostril on each side while sunfishes have two. There are, of course, other differences, but we might be able to generalize by saying that most of the cichlids are to be found in warm water above 65°F. and many of the sunfishes are to be found in cold water below 65°F.

For the aquarist, cichlids may well be the most interesting fishes they have ever met. For the most part they are very hardy and easily spawned, especially fishes of the genera *Aequidens, Cichlasoma, Geophagus, Haplochromis, Apistogramma*, among others. There are also some very popular cichlids which are not so easy to spawn, especially so are the fishes of the genus *Symphysodon* (the discusfish), and wild stocks of the angelfish, *Pterophyllum*. Those cichlids which grow fairly large, over a foot in total length, may also be difficult to spawn in the aquarium only because they are usually stunted by aquarium life and are rarely fed the proper diet. This certainly would describe the oscar, *Astronotus* and *Cichla*, two genera of sportsfish found in South America.

What makes cichlids so interesting to hobbyists and scientists alike is the ethology of cichlid fishes, that is, their behavior. Cichlids are "intelligent" fishes in that they usually have elaborate selective breeding rituals, different color and color patterns to express "attitudes," and they usually can be trained to eat from your hand.

The king of the aquarium world is this *Symphysodon aequifasciata*, the discusfish. Photo by Arend van den Nieuwenhuizen.

How Cichlids Breed

Cichlids, as a family, probably contain species which breed similarly to any way practiced by almost any other fish except the characin *Copeina arnoldi* which lays its eggs outside the water, and some annual fishes which bury their eggs in the mud to estivate over the forthcoming dry season. Cichlids always lay eggs and their eggs are always fairly large. Some cichlids lay eggs which are sticky and adhere to whichever surface they are laid upon. Other cichlids dig a pit in which they lay their eggs and, when they are finished spawning, they gather the eggs in their mouth and incubate them orally (some *Geophagus* and most of the cichlids of the great lakes of Africa). Almost all cichlids guard their young and their eggs against predators, at least until the young can fend for themselves, at which time they either desert them or merely chase them away from the nesting site, gobbling a few of them up in the process. Every cichlid has its own particular spawning ritual, and most of these rituals have very interesting variations. There have been many studies about cichlid behavior and they are a favorite laboratory animal of fish ethologists.

A magnificent series of photographs of *Geophagus balzani* from Paraguay. Upper photo shows the rounded hump formed on the head of an older male. The center photo shows the female over her newly laid eggs. The bottom photos show the female tending the eggs and finally picking them up in her mouth where she stores them until they hatch. Her mouth is also used as a refuge for the young when danger threatens. Photos by Hans Joachim Richter.

A close-up detail of the female acting as a sanctuary for her young. The female can signal the fry to come into her mouth with certain peculiar body language. Photo by Hans Joachim Richter.

A pair of *Aequidens curviceps* as the pair thoroughly clean the rock they have selected for depositing their eggs. Photo by Hans Joachim Richter.

As a model of the typical South American cichlid, let's consider the details involved with a new variety of *Aequidens curviceps*. This new variety is being inbred to develop more and more red in the fish and if you decide to breed this species, be sure to get the most colorful pair you can find and keep selecting those offspring which have more color than their parents, so each successive brood will be more colorful than the previous spawn.

If you are lucky enough to be able to find five or six tank-bred youngsters which are about one inch long (too young to tell which is the male or female), put them into a specially set up tank of at least ten gallons capacity. The tank should be furnished with lots of hiding places, flat stones and perhaps a flowerpot or two laid on its side. These are places for fish to hide should they be chased from another fish's territory. Cichlids, you see, stake a claim on a bit of territory and chase away any other fish which comes into their territory, especially if it's one of their own species. The boundaries are usually imaginary and can only be changed if you move some of the stones and plants around to change their familiar surroundings to an unfamiliar one.

As the fish are cared for with daily feedings of the best foods available, preferably live foods every day with in-between snacks of dried, prepared foods, you should observe those which begin to separate themselves from the crowd. These will normally become males, and as they get older and larger, their dorsal and anal fins will begin to grow longer and more pointed until finally they become more colorful and begin to notice fish of the opposite sex.

Assuming all the fish are from the same age group, the males will get their color and elongated fins at about the time the females begin to bulge with developing eggs. Soon thereafter you will notice that a male and female begin to "want to be alone." The male will have accepted her into his "territory" and they will have begun to clean a smooth, hard flat surface upon which they will deposit their eggs. Sometimes it may be a rock; other times it may be a piece of wood. The accompanying photographs show the pair once having spawned on a rock and once on a flat log. Look closely at both the stone and the log and notice how they have actually polished the area in which they are depositing their eggs!

As soon as the spawning site has been selected and scrubbed, the female will begin to develop a spawning tube (ovipositor) extending from her anal pore. The male's will be visible usually only hours before actual spawning, while the female's will project days ahead of spawning (most of the time).

Finally, the day of spawning has arrived! The female will begin to swim in circles absolutely over the spot she and the male have scrubbed clean. Soon the male will follow her and prepare himself for the spawning ritual. All during this time the pair have isolated themselves and viciously attacked any fish which dared even come close to their spawning site.

After a few "dry runs" over the spawning site, the female will suddenly release a few eggs. During one spawning she first laid three eggs on one side of her 360° course over the spawning site, and then five eggs on the other side. Then she moved away and let the male fertilize the eggs. As soon as he was finished she followed the same route and laid about a dozen eggs, again moving away for the male to fertilize them. As time went on, say five minutes, the fish became so interested in what they were doing that both the male and the female started to swim in circles about each other laying eggs and fertilizing at almost the same time in a head to tail circular motion. In an hour or so, spawning was complete and the pair began a period of incubation not unlike that of a chicken.

The female would usually be the one who would stay "parked" on top of the eggs, perhaps ½ inch above them, waving her pectoral fins in such a manner that water would constantly be passed over the developing eggs, keeping them clean and aerated. The male would be nearby on "guard duty." During certain times the pair would change duties.

During feeding, often both parents would rush for the food, carefully keeping an eye on the eggs. They would almost immediately rush back if another fish showed any interest in their eggs.

The female, as she cleans the spawning site, develops an extended ovipositor through which she will pass her large eggs during the spawning process. The arrow points to the ovipositor which protrudes from her anal pore. Photo by Hans Joachim Richter.

Golden convict cichlids, a tank-raised variety that does not exist in nature! The pair spawned inside this flowerpot and were left with their developing fry without gobbling them up. Allowing cichlids to remain with their fry for more than a few days after the fry are free-swimming is dangerous. Photo by Kasanyi.

The beautiful tank-raised variety of *Aequidens curviceps* in this magnificent series of color photographs shows the step-by-step spawning of cichlids which anchor their eggs in the open. Photos in this series by Hans Joachim Richter.

On the facing page the male makes a final dry run (upper photo) after which the female hovers over the cleaned stone and, with her ovipositor just barely touching the surface, deposits amber eggs in a random pattern. Another color variety of the same fish does the same thing in the two photos on this page.

Swimming in a circular motion, the pair start swimming in tighter and tighter circles as the male fertilizes the eggs even as the female is depositing new ones. Photos by Hans Joachim Richter.

Pretty soon the eggs almost cover the top of the rock which had been so carefully scrubbed clean. The female's ovipositor still extends beyond her body.

During the entire spawning process the male's colors heighten while the female's colors seem to get darker as she nears the end of the spawning. Photos by Hans Joachim Richter.

Finally the female is finished spawning and leaves the spawning site (upper photo) while the male (below) takes complete charge of the eggs and hovers over them, fanning them with his fins to keep them clear of debris and to insure they are properly aerated.

After hatching, the male takes the fry into a previously dug pit in the sand. If you look very closely you can make out the eyes of the mass of fry which are stuck together by fine, sticky threads which extend from their heads.

Not infrequently, if they weren't too hungry, the pair would feed one at a time.

In a few days the eggs would hatch, but in the interim the pair kept a constant vigil over the eggs, inspecting and mouthing them frequently. Those eggs which were not fertilized would have become white and opaque almost immediately and the mouthing action would have broken their delicate shells. The fertilized eggs are much harder and can usually be picked up in your fingers without breaking. This is not recommended, however!

Once the eggs hatch, the male will begin to dig a pit, usually one that is surrounded on at least three sides to act as a corral for the fry. When all the young have hatched, they appear merely as a wriggling mass on top of the spawning site, still attached to the site by a sticky thread attached to their heads. After a few hours of wriggling, the pair will take the fry and move them via their mouths to the pit, where they will be guarded until the fry become free swimming. Sometimes it takes a few days for the young to absorb their yolk sacs and begin swimming freely about looking for food. During this initial free swimming stage, the pair carefully herd the fry in a group, grabbing the strays in their mouths and blowing them back into the school.

This continues until all the fry are free swimming and begin to go hunting for food. Depending upon the pair, the parents may still be allowed to stay with the fry, especially if all the other fish in their nursery tank have been removed. Feedings of freshly hatched brine shrimp or infusoria will be appreciated by the fry and they will grow quickly. If you cannot find the proper food, squeeze the yolk of a hardboiled egg through a fine linen cloth and swish it about the aquarium. The fry will quickly eat these fine particles, but take care that the tank doesn't pollute with the uneaten particles of egg yolk.

Some parents are not as good as others and eat the fry or their eggs at one stage or another. There have been many theories as to why the parents devour their own products, but no one really knows.

During their courtship, the pair will become beautifully colored and they will stay that way until the fry have to be moved. Once they are moved the breeders take on another coloration which is much darker and much more camouflaged.

Not all cichlids breed this way, but most of them do, with such variations as spawning in a cave (imitated by the flowerpot), digging under a rock and spawning upside down under the rock, or choosing a large leaf upon which to deposit their eggs (like many *Pterophyllum* and *Symphysodon*).

There are, however, a group of cichlids which incubate their eggs in their mouths. These fish are usually called "mouthbrooders," and except for the genus *Geophagus* from South America, most of the mouthbrooding cichlids come from Africa.

Mouthbrooders

There are five great lakes in Africa and each has its own very interesting and very diverse fauna. As a matter of fact, in Lakes Tanganyika and Malawi, which I know the best, almost all of the fishes found in these lakes are found nowhere else!

Not all of the fishes in this lake are mouthbrooders by any means, but many are. A typical mouthbrooder from the great lakes of Africa, or for that matter, *Geophagus* from South America, would spawn in the following manner.

A male would usually stake out a territory and build a nest or pit, or, if that wasn't available, he might just clean off a spot on a rock. He would then show his full coloration and dance about the spot, usually spreading his fins, especially his anal fin, to show off what we have become accustomed to calling the "egg spots." When an acceptable female approaches, she will go through a more or less elaborate pre-spawning ritual, until she finally deposits her eggs in the spawning pit. As soon as she lays the first few eggs, the male will hover over them and release sperm to fertilize them. The female will generally then attack the spot where the eggs are located at the same instant the male is fertilizing them, and take the eggs into her mouth. Some fish ethologists say this

As soon as the fry are free-swimming they cluster about the still darkened female. She changes colors with moods. Photos in this series by Hans Joachim Richter.

Pseudotropheus zebra, the B-morph, from Lake Malawi (above) and a pair of *P. tropheops* from Likoma Island (below) shows the egg spots on their anal fin. Photos by the author.

Hemihaplochromis philander female attacking the anal fin of the male during the spawning process. Photo by Rudolf Zukal.

behavior insures that the female gets a mouthful of sperm at the same time because, they say, she keeps pecking at the egg spots on the male's anal fin mistaking them for eggs. This action continues with the female laying more and more eggs until her mouth is full. After each batch of eggs she attacks the male's anal fin, but whether this is just to chase him off the spot or to go after the 'eggs' represented by the egg spots, is uncertain. I, for one, disbelieve the egg spot theory only because I have discovered many mouthbrooders which do not have egg spots in their anal fins, and many mouthbrooders which have egg spots in fins other than their anal fins! After a considerable amount of diving in the great lakes of Africa, I have found that the egg spots seem to be used for identification, for the males always do most of their displaying in fairly dark areas, isolated from the other fishes. Perhaps the females need this color pattern to be "turned on?"

In any case, the female is usually the one to keep the eggs in her mouth until they hatch (but once in a while the male takes on this chore. . . which is additional evidence against the egg spot theory). Hatching may take a few days and, of course, during that time the female doesn't eat. Once the eggs hatch, the female still protects her young and she becomes a swimming sanctuary for them. At the slightest provocation of danger, they dash back for the safety of her mouth, staying there until danger has passed.

The number of fry that can fit into a female's mouth is amazing.

The African cichlids, by the way, especially those from the great lakes, usually have fewer eggs than the South American cichlids. If you want to learn a lot more about African cichlids, get a copy of my book *African Cichlids of Lakes Malawi and Tanganyika*.

The Discus and the Angelfish

If you read the older aquarium books, especially those written in the early years of our hobby around 1920, you will find that the writers often considered both angelfish and discusfish of equal difficulty in spawning. Through the years, as the angelfish were inbred, generation after generation, they became easier and easier to spawn, since those fish which were difficult to spawn just would be put aside in favor of those which were easier to spawn. Actually this was a process of selective breeding for ease of spawning.

The same process is going on with discusfish. In the 1950's it was a great event to spawn discus; nowadays, while it is far from a common occurrence, it is almost a daily happening, especially in commercial hatcheries which specialize in discus.

To prove the point, there has recently (1972) been a massive importation of wild angelfish. Among the newly imported fishes were the magnificent *Pterophyllum altum*, the largest of all angelfishes. Almost every professional breeder in Europe and America has tried to breed these wild fish, but as yet not one of them has succeeded!

Pterophyllum dumerilii from the Purus River in Brazil. Photo by Dr. Herbert R. Axelrod.

Pterophyllum altum, the largest of the angelfish from South America. Photo by the author in the aquarium of Heiko Bleher.

One of the freaks which appeared among the angelfish was this marbled sport, which became a fixed strain. The appearance of various different sports and the ability of aquarists to fix these strains has made fortunes for some breeders. Photo by Hans Joachim Richter.

Unquestionably, millions of angelfish have been bred in captivity. As a result, many varieties have been developed by constant inbreeding of the "freaks" which appear as sports among otherwise normal batches of fry. In nature these freaks would not be able to compete and would die or be eaten. But in the aquarium the loving hand of the breeder intervenes and isolates the freak in order to fix the apparent difference to make a new variety. As a result, the usual striped silver angelfish is now available in solid silver (the blushing or ghost angelfish), solid black, almost solid black (black lace), gold and albino. Combinations of all colors and fin shapes also exist. Thus there is such a fish as a veil-tailed marble angelfish! Soon we might even see a solid red angelfish. . . although I doubt that we'll ever see a solid blue one.

Facing page: golden convict cichlids feeding from a freeze-dried tubifex worm feeding bell with cardinal tetras as tank mates. The cichlids had to be kept well fed or they would have made a meal out of the tetras. Photo by the author.

Feeding Cichlids

Most cichlids are omnivorous; that is, they will eat almost anything from algae to other fishes to worms and shrimp. In nature, of course, cichlids have evolved in some cases into specialists preferring to eat either algae or other fishes or worms, etc. Some species in the great lakes of Africa even specialize in such nasty tactics as eating eyeballs, or, in some cases, eating scales. One cichlid even seeks out mouthbrooders with their mouths full of eggs or fry; when the victim is found, the predator grasps the hapless victim by the snout and forces the mouthbrooder to spit the eggs or fry into its own mouth, where they become a meal!

Such are the habits of cichlids. Is it any wonder they are such favorites among the true tropical fish hobbyists?

This is a bleeding heart angelfish. The transparency of the operculum and the lack of pigmentation in the scales and skin gives the operculum a reddish tinge which prompted the name bleeding heart. This is, of course, a tank-bred variety and does not exist in nature. Photo by Rudolf Zukal.

A basically normally colored angelfish but one whose fins have grown extremely long. This character was fixed and the strain called veiltail angelfish. Photo by the author.

"Albino" angelfish developed by Karl Naja of Milwaukee, Wisconsin. These fish have black eyes which turn red when the fish is mature. Photo by the author.

Zebra angelfish, still another new strain, appeared on the aquarium scene in late 1973. The entire body is blotched and spotted seemingly in a regular pattern, especially in the fins. Photo by Dr. Herbert R. Axelrod.

Symphysodon aequifasciata haraldi is the blue discus which has the red stripes wider than the blue stripes on the back. Photo by the author.

The two discusfish shown above were collected by the author in March, 1974 near Lake Tefe in Brazil. They are *Symphysodon aequifasciata aequifasciata*, the green discus. Note that the green or blue markings are wider than the red interstitial areas. In the photo below is *Symphysodon aequifasciata haraldi*, in which the interstitial areas are wider than the blue stripes. Upper photos by the author; lower photo by Dr. D. Terver, Nancy Aquarium.

A close-up of the head of the green discus collected by the author in the waters surrounding Lake Tefe, Brazil in March, 1974. Note the green color for which these discusfish are famed. If you see the markings on the head and notice that the green stripes are thicker than the interstitial red markings, you can recognize the fish as *Symphysdon aequifasciata aequifasciata*. Photo by the author.

One of the local natives of Lake Tefe poses with the discus we collected in her nearby lake. The lake is shown on the facing page. Photo by Dr. Martin Brittan.

The author handling a net which is used to collect small fishes which hide in dense bushes or grass. The trees in the background harbored lots of green discus in this lake near Tefe, Brazil. Photo by Dr. Martin Brittan.

The tree in the middle of this photograph, near Tefe, Brazil, was the home of a discus family. Discus like to stay near trees which are submerged during the high water season. Photo by the author.

This beautiful lake is overflowing and it is filled not only with discusfish but also with hundreds of other species from piranhas to catfish. This lake is a blackwater lake connected to Rio Tefe. Photo by the author.

Symphysodon aequifasciata axelrodi, the brown discus, is characterized by having very few markings on its back and forehead. The fish was named to honor the author by Dr. Leonard P. Schultz. Photo by the author.

Dr. Eduard Schmidt-Focke of Frankfurt, Germany is the world's leading discus breeder. He took this photo many years ago to show the fry eating the slime from the body of their parents.

The turquoise discus developed by Jack Wattley and distributed by Jack Roberts of Roberts Fish Farm, Miami, Florida is probably derived from the green discus from Tefe, *Symphysodon aequifasciata aequifasciata*.

The real discus, *Symphysodon discus*, shows three heavy markings. There is one through the eye, one in the middle of its body and one at the base of the tail.

This royal blue discus is the true discus species, *Symphysodon discus*. Photo by Dr. D. Terver at the Nancy Aquarium, Nancy, France.

This is a tank-raised discus, probably from *Symphysodon discus* parents. Photo by Wolfgang Bechtle.

A male *Aequidens itanyi* from South America. Photo by Rudolf Zukal.

Aequidens pulcher spawning on a flat stone. Photo by Rudolf Zukal.

Aequidens maronii spawning. Photo by Arend van den Nieuwenhuizen.

Aequidens portalegrensis, male. Photo by Hansen.

A male dwarf cichlid, *Apistogramma agassizi*, from South America. During spawning the fish becomes much more colorful. Photo by Hans Joachim Richter.

A pair of dwarf cichlids, *Nannacara anomala* spawning. The male has the more intense coloration and hovers over the female as she lays her eggs. Photo by Rudolf Zukal.

Apistogramma reitzigi is another dwarf cichlid from South America. This one looks like a cave spawner as the female lays her eggs upside down in a cave. The male waits for her to finish so he can fertilize the eggs. Note how spread out the eggs are. This indicates an inexperienced female. Photo by Rudolf Zukal.

Apistogramma are the most beautiful of the dwarf cichlids. This fish is known in the trade as *Apistogramma sweglesi*, but the author has not been able to verify that name. This is a male in breeding color. Photo by Hans Joachim Richter.

A male *Apistogramma corumbae*. Photo by Arend van den Nieuwenhuizen.

A golden *Apistogramma ramirezi* male displaying in front of a normally colored female as she prepares to lay more eggs. Photo by Hans Joachim Richter.

A male *Apistogramma ortmanni*, a well known dwarf cichlid from South America. Photo by Klaus Paysan.

The two fish shown in the photos below are a male and female *Apistogramma borelli*. The less colorful of the two is the female. These photographs were taken by Hans Joachim Richter in 1967. I'm sure you will agree that his photographic skills have increased considerably since that time.

Apistogramma pertense is a beautiful dwarf cichlid which ranges along the Amazon from Manaus east to Santarem. The fish was first described in 1911 by Hasemann when specimens were brought into Germany by aquarist-sailors who made their way up the Amazon River hauling rubber. Photo by Hans Joachim Richter.

Apistogramma wickleri is a magnificent small cichlid from South America that was named to honor the great fish behaviorist Wolfgang Wickler. This pair, with the male in front, are spawning in a cave made from a coconut shell. Note the red eggs! The female is spawning upside down. Photo by Hans Joachim Richter.

Cichlasoma festivum ranges over most of the Amazon River system and probably even farther than that. This is a male as evidenced by his longer and more pointed anal and dorsal fins. Photo by Rudolf Zukal.

Cichlasoma coryphaenoides is neither as peaceful nor as small as the fish above. This is a male. Photo by Hansen.

This is an old *Cichlasoma octofasciatum*, also known as the Jack Dempsey because the fish is so aggressive. Photo by Dr. Stanislav Frank.

Cichlasoma meeki, the firemouth cichlid, guarding their free-swimming fry. These fish originally came from Mexico but are so easily bred that no one bothers to import them any more. Photo by Rudolf Zukal.

Cichlasoma nigrofasciatum. This photograph shows a male guarding his developing eggs. The eggs are about a day old, as evidenced by the white caps developing on the end. Photo by Rudolf Zukal.

The famous Texas cichlid, *Cichlasoma cyanoguttatum*, is the only cichlid found in the United States. It spawns very readily in the springtimc. Photo by K. Paysan.

In 1963 Harald Schultz discovered this small *Aequidens* which was never brought back alive. No one has described the fish, so it has no name. Photo by Harald Schultz.

A fish which looks similar to the one above and is for some reason is called the dolphin cichlid is another undescribed *Aequidens* species. Photo by Aaron Norman.

The many faces of *Cichlasoma severum* are shown in this montage by Wolfgang Bechtle. The fish lock jaws as a test in their mate selection. The male guards the eggs in the smaller photo to the middle right.

Ever since the great naturalist Heckel described the discusfish and *Cichlasoma severum* at the same time in 1840, aquarists and scientists alike have always linked the two fishes. As a matter of fact the juveniles of the two are extremely similar and both are gentle, peaceful fish. Just as there are many different color varieties and races of discusfish, so are there many races and varieties of *C. severum*. But while Dr. Leonard Schultz spént some time studying discusfish, no one has bothered to study *C. severum*. I collected this male from the Rio Aguaro, Venezuela in 1971. Photo by the author.

A golden strain of *Cichlasoma severum* has been developed; while they certainly are similar in some ways to *Cichlasoma severum*, their basic color markings and the shape of their head indicate further comparisons are necessary. Photo by Barbara E. Marlay.

The fish on the top of the page was five inches; this specimen from Guyana (1965) was three inches. It must be assumed that since both are wild fish, the larger one would be older than the smaller one, yet the principle that the bars (except the last two) disappear as the fish gets older may not hold. Photo by the author.

This is still another color variety of the fish called *Cichlasoma severum.* It is spotted and blotched and does not have the black bar across the caudal peduncle. Photo by Aaron Norman.

A pair of breeding *Cichlasoma severum* as they lay their eggs on a flat stone. While the bars on the male seem to be faded, the fish to the rear has distinct bars. Photo by Rudolf Zukal.

Not all cichlids are sunfish-shaped. . . and not all are peaceful and quiet like the angelfish, discus and *C.. severum*. Some fish in the family Cichlidae are mean and predatory, and this is especially true of the pike cichlids. The fish to the right is *Crenicichla dorsocellata*, which has a very wide range over the entire Amazon. Photo by Harald Schultz.

While collecting in the Rio Aguaro, Venezuela in 1971, I found many cichlids and, as is my usual practice, I put them all into plastic bags until I could sort them out and photograph them. Imagine my surprise when I found that a *Crenicichla lepidota* had gobbled up one of my new species of *Aequidens* and choked to death on it! *Crenicichla lepidota* was described in 1840 by Heckel . . . the same year as the discus and *C. severum*! Photo by the author.

Crenicara maculata is a dwarf cichlid which has a name and shape similar to those of the *Crenicichla* species, but what a difference! They are kind, gentle and intelligent fishes which are highly recommended for the home aquarist. Photo by Klaus Paysan.

Geophagus in Latin or Greek means something like "earth-eater." That's exactly what these shovel-faced fish do. They eat the gravel in their aquarium, straining out whatever they can find. It is interesting that Heckel described this species in 1840 too! Actually *Geophagus jurupari*, the fish to the left, is very widely distributed all over northern South America and has been a hit with aquarists because it is so peaceful (relatively) and can be kept in most tanks even though it continually chews up the gravel. Photo by Hansen.

The Rio Aguaro produced these *Geophagus daemon*, a very beautiful fish, though one that is completely unknown for aquarium purposes. The black spots on the fins are parasites. Photo by the author.

A close-up of the head of a typical eartheater, *Geophagus surinamensis*, which ranges over the northern Amazon region to Guyana and Venezuela. The black parasites are similar to those on *Geophagus daemon* (see facing page), and the author collected them both from Rio Aguaro, Venezuela. Photo by Dr. Herbert R. Axelrod.

In all of Asia there are only a few cichlids and these belong to the genus *Etroplus*. The South American and African continents have hundreds, even thousands, of species, while Asia has but two or three; these probably swam over from Africa, since *Etroplus* has quite a tolerance for sea water. The photograph above shows the yellow strain of *Etroplus maculatus* guarding their fry in a shallow pit they dug in the gravel. Photo by Rudolf Zukal.

One of the rare and very desirable cichlids from Brazil is *Uaru amphiacanthoides*. The word "*uaru*" is a Brazilian Indian word, and no one knows the meaning except that this is the name of the fish! The fry and juveniles change colors dramatically. This photo was taken by Dr. D. Terver at the Nancy Aquarium. The photo below shows one-inch-long juveniles spawned and photographed in Japan by H. Azuma.

The continent of Africa is blessed with a large genus of fishes called *Haplochromis*. The genus is broken down into subgenera according to various ichthyologists, but essentially the genus *Haplochromis* is becoming more and more popular as fishes from the great lakes of Africa (Malawi, Tanganyika, Victoria, etc.) become available. The first and perhaps most popular of all *Haplochromis*-type fishes is the Egyptian mouthbrooder, *Hemihaplochromis multicolor*. This photo was taken by H. Hansen at the Berlin Aquarium.

A similar fish from central Africa is *Hemihaplochromis philander*. This is a male shown in display attitude. Photo by Rudolf Zukal.

Hemichromis fasciatus is another African cichlid which is found throughout central west Africa. It reaches 12 inches in length and is a food fish. Because it is so quarrelsome, it is not recommended for the community aquarium. Normally the sides are decorated with five dark black blotches; they are faded in this specimen. Photo by the author.

There are many other dwarf cichlids in Africa, and many of the genus *Pelvicachromis* are both peaceful and colorful, two prime requisites for an aquarium. The fish above is *Pelvicachromis roloffi*. Photo by E. Roloff. The fish below is of a closely related genus, *Nanochromis*. The species is *N. dimidiatus*. Photo by Hans Joachim Richter.

One of the most widespread of all African cichlids might very well be *Hemichromis bimaculatus*, which was originally described by Gill in 1862. The jewelfish, as it is called, ranges over the three major river systems of Africa, namely the Nile, Niger and the Congo. In each river system it has more or less red coloration. The fish shown here is the Congo jewelfish, sometimes even referred to as "*Hemichromis bimaculatus* II." It is the most red of all the races. The photo below shows the pair laying their eggs on a flat stone. The two photos on the right are close-ups of the male (upper photo) and the female (lower photo) as they actually spawn. This remarkable sequence of photos by Hans Joachim Richter.

Pelvicachromis taeniatus was described by Boulenger in 1901 based upon specimens from West Africa. Both sexes are highly colored, and the eye spots or ocelli are visible in both males and females. These are very peaceful fish and make ideal additions to the home aquarium. Photo by Hansen.

Pelvicachromis pulcher was also described by Boulenger in 1901, though he originally classified it as a *Pelmatochromis*. It is found in the Niger delta and is a very beautiful and desirable species of dwarf African cichlid. Photo by Kremser.

Nanochromis nudiceps was described by Boulenger in 1899 from the Stanley Pool outside of Kinshasa, Zaire. It is not exceptionally beautiful, but it has a very distinguished air of superiority and intelligence so common with dwarf cichlids. This photo by Hans Joachim Richter shows the pair escorting their free-swimming fry.

From the great lakes of Africa come some of the most interesting cichlids in the world. These lakes (there are five of them and some of my most pleasurable days were spent diving and collecting in these lakes) contain cichlids found, for the most part, in the lakes and nowhere else. *A Labeotropheus trewavasae* male is shown to the left.

A beautiful color variety, found in Lake Malawi, of the popular *Labeotropheus trewavasae*. This fish was named to honor Dr. Ethelwyn Trewavas of the British Museum of Natural History for all the work she has done on African cichlids. Photo by Dr. Herbert R. Axelrod.

Labeotropheus fuelleborni, another beautiful fish from Lake Malawi. Photo by Dr. D. Terver.

An aerial view of Lake Malawi near Monkey Bay. Each island in the lake has its own basic race of fishes. Note the rocks along the coast. These rocks continue down into the water and serve as an ideal habitat for cichlid fishes. Photo by the author.

These two underwater photographs were taken by the author in about 25 feet depth near Cape McClear, Lake Malawi. The rocks are covered with a rich growth of algae known as "*aufwuchs*" upon which most of the cichlids constantly graze. The water in Lake Malawi (and Lake Tanganyika for that matter) is crystal clear. . . much clearer than on many of the coral atolls, and the fishes are friendly, so they pose readily for the underwater camera bug! A visit to Lake Malawi is very enjoyable and extremely worthwhile for the cichlid lover.

Many of the Malawian cichlids have color varieties found in different parts of the lake. The fish to the left is the OB (orange blotched) morph of *Pseudotropheus zebra*. This is a wild fish just collected. As with many of the other Malawian cichlids, it seems to have a chunk taken out of its tail. Photo by the author.

This is the O (orange) morph of *Pseudotropheus zebra* found in the same lake but in a different locale from the one above. Photo by the author.

One of the most beautiful of the rift lake cichlids of Africa is *Haplochromis moori*. This photo of a beautiful male shows him just beginning the to grow the lump on his forehead which is typical of the species. Photo by Hansen, at Berlin Aquarium, Berlin, Germany.

A new species of *Labidochromis* yet to be described. The fish was collected by Peter and Henny Davies in Lake Malawi. I photographed it in an aquarium in the lobby of the Monkey Bay Hotel in Monkey Bay, on the lake. The *Sagittaria* plant comes from the lake. The photograph at the bottom of this page was taken in the same tank.

Pseudotropheus auratus in its normal color; this is a newly caught fish in Lake Malawi. Photo by the author.

Melanochromis sp. (probably *vermivorus*) from Lake Malawi. These rift lake cichlids are fascinating to keep, though they are very territorial and require a large tank with lots of hiding places. Photo by the author.

From the middle of Lake Tanganyika, the home of many rare cichlids, I took this photo across to the mountains of Zaire (Congo), from whose hills the soldiers took potshots at us, seemingly for target practice!

Underwater, in about 30 feet, I was able to get this photo of a pair of *Cyphotilapia frontosa* in their typical habitat. In the photo below, again in Lake Tanganyika but in only 15 feet of water, you can see the density of fishes, especially the *Julidochromis* and *Lamprologus brichardi*.

A pair of *Lamprologus brichardi* (formerly called *Lamprologus savoryi elongatus*) spawning. Note the pink eggs (about a dozen of them) on the side of the mottled rock to which the lower fish is attending! Pierre Brichard exports thousands of these fishes every year from Bujumbura, Burundi. Photo by Hans Joachim Richter.

Julidochromis is a genus of rock-inhabiting species from Lake Tanganyika. They squeeze into the small cracks in the rocks, and collecting them is very difficult with the use of anesthesia or electric-shock equipment. There is some question about the real variability of the fish shown on the left and the one shown below. Both may be color varieties of *Julidochromis marlieri*. Photo by Dr. Robert Goldstein.

Julidochromis ornatus is a magnificent species from Lake Tanganyika. Hans Joachim Richter spawned these fish, and this photo is one shot from the spawning sequence which appears in my book *African Cichlids of Lakes Malawi and Tanganyika*.

Tropheus moorii is a mouthbrooder from Lake Tanganyika that is supposed to have very large eggs! I wonder if they are as large as those of the chocolate gourami? This is a very beautiful and most desired fish. Photo by the author.

Cyphotilapia frontosa just beginning to show the lump on the forehead from which its "*frontosa*" name derived. Photo by H. Hansen at the Berlin Aquarium, Berlin, Germany.

In about 30 feet of water in Lake Tanganyika, I watched a pair of *Cyathopharynx furcifer* spawning/flirting. The male is ranging over a pit he dug in the sand. He dances in front of every female that comes by until he finds one that will spawn in his nest. The fish is the foreground is *Cyphotilapia frontosa*. Photo by the author.

THE CATFISHES

Dianema longibarbis is a beautiful catfish collected by the author in the small, milky pond shown in the photograph below. We found the pond near Capivara, Tefe, Brazil and in the same pond we found thousands of *Corydoras nanus*, a small catfish. Photos by the author.

THE CATFISHES

What makes a catfish a catfish? The whiskers, of course! Someone once thought that every fish which had whiskers looked like a cat and, therefore, should be called a catfish. This generalization is far from true, for while most catfishes have whiskers, not every fish with whiskers is a catfish.

I guess that the catfishes are the most variable group of fishes in the world. They are found almost universally where other fishes exist and they show many adaptations that are found in almost no other fishes.

Some catfishes, such as some of those in the family Mochokidae which range all over Africa except the desert, swim upside down at times (some *Synodontis*). These mochokids are very popular with aquarists even though they grow rather large, are naked in that they do not have scales, scutes or body "armor" of any kind, and are usually very expensive, since all are imported from Africa. No one has commercially spawned any of the African catfishes, even though they do very well in captivity. I remember well how Pierre Brichard took me to the Stanley Pool outside the city then called Leopoldville in the Belgian Congo, now Kinshasa, Zaire. It was late evening when we prepared to collect the catfishes which come out of hiding at night to feed. We had a seine 50 feet long and about 8 feet high. One pull of the seine from the beach of the local yacht club and we had thousands of upside-down catfish, *Synodontis nigriventris*. Since this species has serrated dorsal and pectoral spines which the fish lock in an extended position when taken from the water, we spent the rest of the night carefully removing the fish from the net, where they had become helplessly entwined with the quarter-inch mesh. It might have been a lot easier to cut

Corydoras aeneus, which has a very wide range over South America, is probably the most commonly known *Corydoras* species. Here we see a female carrying some eggs between her ventral fins. Immediately above her caudal peduncle she has previously pasted an egg. In the two photos below, photographer Giancarlo Padovanni has captured part of the spawning ritual of albino *Corydoras aeneus*.

off these stout spines with cutting pliers, but Brichard said that if you break the spine, the fin would fungus and the fish would ultimately perish.

For the aquarist, the most common catfishes are those from South America in the family Callichthyidae, the mailed catfishes. These are small fish which get their "mailed" name from the two rows of bony plates which overlap like the armor of one of King Arthur's knights. Most of the fishes in this family have very strong spines in their dorsal, adipose, pectoral and pelvic fins. The serration on the pectoral spines may be highly variable from species to species, especially in the genus *Corydoras*, and the author finds this characteristic extremely useful in identification.

There is no generalization about where these *Corydoras* fishes can be found. I have found them in stagnant pools by the millions. As a matter of fact when you find them in stagnant pools you always find hundreds of thousands of them jammed into a minimal space. I have also found them in huge rivers and shallow, fast-moving streams and almost within 100 yards of the Atlantic Ocean.

Most callichthyids require access to the air to supplement their gills with an occasional "drink" of air which is utilized and absorbed in their lower digestive tract. *Corydoras* and *Dianema* as well as the other members of this family often swim rapidly to the surface of the water for a gulp of air.

Not all members of the family breed in the same manner. The *Corydoras*, which are exported from almost every country in South America east of the Andes Mountains, have a very elaborate spawning ritual which is still not fully understood. Basically a pair or group of *Corydoras* join in a spawning orgy. The males and females swim about one another, with the female repeatedly attacking the male's vent. It

Burkhard Kahl made this wonderful photo montage of the most common species of *Corydoras* catfishes from South America. There are probably about 100 species of *Corydoras* known to aquarists. From top to bottom, left to right: first row, all *Corydoras*, (1) *C. paleatus*, (2) *C. schwartzi*, (3) *C. julii*, (4) *C. melanistius;* second row, (5) *C. arcuatus*, (6) *C. myersi*, (7) *C. aeneus*, (8) *C. aeneus schultzi;* bottom row, (9) *C. punctatus*, (10) *Brochis coeruleus*, related to *Corydoras* but a different genus, (11) *C. hastatus* and (12) a pair of *C. hastatus*, supposedly a subspecies.

From the Rio Magdelena in Colombia comes this beautiful *Corydoras metae*. This variety has a solid black dorsal fin; other varieties have less black in the dorsal. Photo by the author.

Three spotted *Corydoras* which vary tremendously in size, from front to rear: *Corydoras julii, Corydoras punctatus punctatus* and *Corydoras melanistius*. Photo by the author.

Brazil exports thousands of *Dianema urostriata* every year, though the fish is far from a favorite! I find it very beautiful and call it the flagtail catfish. Photo by the author.

An unidentified loricariid catfish. Photo by Harald Schultz.

Otocinclus affinis. Photo by Harald Schultz.

Hypostomus plecostomus. Photo by Aaron Norman.

Callichthys callichthys. Photo by Aaron Norman.

Xenocara dolichoptera.

A rare catfish, an albino *Hypostomus plectostomus*. Top photo is a bottom view of the same fish shown below. Photos by the author.

is strongly suggestive of her receiving sperm in her mouth, since further activity indicates no other contact with the male.

Once she has made a contact with the male's vent, she soon discharges a few eggs which she clasps in her ventral fins. At this time the ventral fins almost fuse into a cup which looks very much like a pair of cupped human hands. The female then swims about the tank with her eggs clasped between her ventrals looking for a suitable place to deposit her eggs. More often than not she lays the eggs on the front glass of the aquarium, but she may also choose a heater tube or a strong leaf. She seems to mouth the area upon which she will deposit her sticky eggs. It is theorized that at this time she has already spat out the sperm and merely presses the eggs into position on top of the sperm. The eggs are laid randomly in small groups all over the aquarium.

Callichthys and *Dianema* spawn much differently. They build a bubble-nest under a floating log or large leaf and spawn under the nest, with the floating eggs being tended by the male. The eggs hatch in about five days, after which the male should be removed and the young raised alone.

There are many other families of catfishes of interest to aquarists. The suckermouth catfishes of the family Loricariidae are also of interest to aquarists because of the algae-eating characteristics of this family. While the Callichthyidae were characterized by two rows of bony scutes arranged laterally along the flanks, this family has three or four rows, with some even having their ventral surface covered with this same armor. *Hypostomus* (*Plecostomus*), *Xenocara, Loricaria, Farlowella, Otocinclus* and *Ancistrus* are just some of the loricariids which are imported regularly for aquarists from many South American countries. They are much more difficult to breed than the *Corydoras* or *Callichthys* catfishes, and no one is commercially spawning any of the loricariids.

Most loricariids spawn in tunnels or tubes, and a few (*Loricaria, Ancistrus*) lay eggs which they incubate almost like a mother hen. The *Hypostomus* or *Plecostomus* species have huge (usually red) eggs which make good

I photographed this fish in Brichard's compound in Kinshasa in 1969. It is one of the many beautiful African catfishes and is known as *Synodontis flavitaeniatus*.

I was able to photograph a very lovely spotted catfish which Thierry Brichard, the son of Pierre, had collected from Lake Tanganyika. The fish is a lovely silver and is endowed with strong, fleshy barbels. It has been identified as *Synodontis nigromaculatus* by Dr. Max Poll. The photo below is a close-up of the face of this same fish.

caviar. Big suckermouth catfishes are a main source of food in the Amazon, and in the early days (prior to 1960) regular boats carrying thousands of these fishes ran up and down the Amazon supplying live fish to local markets where the people would buy them alive and roast them over a hot fire. The flesh is boneless and tastes very much like lobster.

Catfishes, as a rule, are very hardy and adaptable. Most are nocturnal and do best in subdued light.

An unidentified upside-down catfish from Africa is this *Synodontis* species lying upside-down under a rock. Photo by Klaus Paysan.

Klaus Paysan also took this photo of *Synodontis schall*, which has some very fine spots that are hardly visible in this rather dark photograph.

From Lake Malawi I was able to photograph *Synodontis nyassae*, a lovely spotted catfish whose extended belly indicates it had a good meal before it ended up in my wax-based examination tray! Photo by the author.

Brichard collected this golden *Synodontis multipunctatus* which I photographed in his compound in Bujumbura, Burundi on the banks of Lake Tanganyika.

Synodontis alberti is a Congo fish collected by Brichard in the Congo and photographed by the author in Brichard's Congo compound in Kinshasa in 1969.

The trade confuses this fish, *Synodontis petricola*, with the fish above. Photo by the author of a fish collected by Brichard in Burundi.

This fish is more often found upside-down, but here I found him right-side up; it is *Synodontis contractus* from the Congo. Photo by the author in Brichard's Kinshasa compound, 1969.

At one time this upside-down catfish was known as *Synodontis davidi*, but additional research has shown it to be just a color variety of the fish shown on page 269 as *Synodontis contractus*. The photograph below shows a close-up of the underside of this same fish. Photos by the author.

Dr. E. Balon's book on *Fishes of Lake Kariba, Africa* contains photographs of fishes never seen before by any aquarist. This catfish, *Synodontis nebulosus*, is one of Dr. Balon's contributions to aquatic photography.

In the Congo River you might find this small *Synodontis nummifer*. They grow considerably larger than the one shown. Photo by the author in the Congo. Fish collected by Pierre Brichard.

Unquestionably the most beautiful of all catfish from Africa is *Synodontis angelicus*, the spotted catfish found throughout the Congo River in very limited quantities. Being nocturnal in habit, the fish is hard to collect and hardly worth the effort, since it hides most of the time in the aquarium anyway. Photo by Aaron Norman.

The shovelnosed catfish is not for the small aquarium. It grows very large and gobbles up everything it sees! Photo by Hansen at the Berlin Aquarium of a 12-inch long *Sorubim lima*. The fish grows at least twice as long as this one and is a major food fish along the Amazon. Bloch and Schneider described the fish in 1806.

From the Congo comes this little beauty, *Etropiella debauwi*. Photo by the author.

Pimelodella gracilis comes from South America and is very common, especially at night.

The glass catfish from southeast Asia, *Kryptopterus macrocephalus*. Photo by Douglas Faulkner.

The photo to the left and the two spotted catfish in the two photos above are the very famous electric catfish from Africa, *Malapterurus electricus*. It is a fat, sluggish fish not worth its own aquarium in anyone's home. The lower fish in the center photograph is *Heterobranchus longifilis*. These photos are by Dr. Eugene Balon from his book, *Fishes of Lake Kariba, Africa.*

THE LIVEBEARERS

Central America and the Caribbean Islands such as Haiti, Cuba and the Bahamas are the range of a series of livebearing fishes, most of which are silvery, feed from the top mostly on insects, and are sexually different in that the males have their anal fins modified into an intromittent organ of reproduction. *Poecilia melanogaster* is shown here. Photo by Rudolf Zukal.

LIVEBEARERS

Of all the aquarium fishes, those which give birth to living young are probably the most popular of all. Many millions of mollies, platies, swordtails and guppies are sold each year to beginners. There are hundreds of fish farms in Florida, Singapore, Hong Kong and Bangkok which turn out so many of these colorful, easy to keep, easy to breed fishes that several million dollars in air freight charges are spent just to get them to their respective markets.

It is interesting that the livebearers I mentioned above are all American fishes! Most originate in Mexico (the platies and swordtails), some in the United States (the mollies) and the guppy probably originated in Trinidad, though it has been so spread around that it is undoubtedly the most common wild fish to be found in Singapore at the present time.

Livebearing is not limited to the small, toy fishes which we know in pet shops. Many of the larger fishes like rays and sharks also may give birth to living young, as may some snakes! But in most cases this livebearing capability has little comparison with mammalian livebearing. With most fishes, especially the tropical toy fishes, fertilization takes place through the modified anal fin of the male, which shoots packets of sperm into the body of the female, where internal fertilization of the eggs take place. The female then merely acts as a home for the developing eggs; she does not give the developing eggs any food, nor is her body chemistry (blood, etc.) connected with the developing fry. Once the eggs have developed sufficiently, and this usually takes about 28 days, the young are discharged and go swimming away. If she gives birth in a separate nursery tank which is heavily laden with fine-leaved plants, her young have a good chance at survival. If she releases her young in a community tank, chances are that the fry will be gobbled up by the other fishes almost as soon as they are released! Since female fishes get fatter as their eggs develop internally, it is a good idea to set up separate nursery tanks in which the female can give birth and the young can be raised.

Another important feature of livebearers from the point of view of the aquarist is that the fish are hardy and are easily bred. This means that you can practice genetics by crossing different color varieties of the same species, or, as you become more skilled, you might be able to cross different species, especially closely related species such as the platies and swordtails. No one has really demonstrated that mollies could be crossed with guppies, or that swordtails and platies might be crossed with either mollies or guppies. But you can try!

Then, too, as you observe your mollies, swordtails, platies and guppies, you might find an offspring that has some interesting physical characteristic which you might like to "fix" into a strain. Almost all the livebearers that are available at pet shops today are the result of mutants or sports which were observed in normal litters of fish. In nature these freaks would probably not survive, so chances of finding them are almost nil. But in the aquarium where a particular fish can be given the best of care and protection, everything is possible. Just think of the many different color varieties of swordtails and platies. Or just think of how many different kinds of guppies there are. Maybe you'll be lucky enough to find some strange freak in your own batch of babies.

In a book of this sort too much attention cannot be given to any single group of fishes, but there are plenty of books, mostly at your local pet shop (very few book stores carry specialized fish books) which cover every aquarium livebearer. Look through some of the books and if one group of fishes interests you most, study about them. Livebearers are easy. . . and they are a lot of fun. . . and profit.

The small silvery fishes that all look so much alike are all various "mosquito" fishes not because they are as small as mosquitoes, but because they have been utilized to eat mosquito larvae when they hatched in the water. As a result, *Gambusia* have been introduced all over the world as a means of mosquito control.

Guppies do not exist in nature like the ones shown on this page! This is a fancy male prizewinning fish bred by Dale Marteeny; the photo is by Midge Hill. The photograph below is one of Rudolf Zukal's fancy snakeskin guppies. Taken in Czechoslovakia, it shows that the Eastern bloc nations go in more for color than for long fins.

In the late 1960's a beautiful strain of bleeding heart platies was developed in Florida by Joseph Cooley, who had a fish farm near Tampa. These are three males which show the variation in color common in this strain. Photo by Dr. Herbert R. Axelrod.

Dr. Myron Gordon, who died some years ago, was my teacher. He developed the use of fishes for the study of human cancer inheritance, and he favored the platies and swordtails for this work. The fish shown above are blue wagtail platies. The male is the upper and smaller fish. Compare the marks on the caudal peduncle of these two fish. Notice the female has a blue-black pattern which if she were turned on her head might look like a Mickey Mouse outline. This blackness might turn into a cancer called a melanoma. Photo by the author.

This species of platy is the same as that on the facing page. It, too, was developed by Dr. Gordon and it was called the salt-and-pepper platy by the Florida fish farmers who grew it. The black spots on this fish rarely develop cancer. The anal fin of the female (upper fish) is easily seen in this photo. Compare it to the gonopodium (modified anal fin) of the male. Photo by the author.

George Graves of Florida developed these beautiful variatus platies (*Xiphophorus variatus*) which had the color of marigolds. Since his wife's name was Mary, he proposed to call these fish marigold platies. The center fish is the female. It is not usual that a female has as much color as the male in *X. variatus*. Photo by the author.

Ten years after Graves developed the marigold platy, someone was able to transfer the beautiful characteristics to a swordtail, and thus the marigold swordtail became a reality. Of course this was done by crossing a marigold platy with a swordtail. Platies and swordtails interbreed easily in the aquarium. Photo by Dr. Herbert R. Axelrod.

Blood red swordtails are the most sought after color variety. The intensity of the red and the length of the tail in the male seem to be contrasting characteristics. That is, the more red in the fish, the shorter the sword! The female is the top fish. Photo by the author.

Dr. Gordon developed the wagtail pattern; he put it onto this very deep red swordtail and came up with the blood red wagtail swordtail. Photo by the author.

Dr. Myron Gordon developed a black marking, which he called tuxedo, on the sides of swordtails. Thus his red swordtails were dressed up with a tuxedo and became red tuxedo swordtails. Males of this strain have very long tails because the red color is weak. Photo by Dr. Herbert R. Axelrod.

Since Dr. Gordon's death there haven't been many new color varieties of platyfish, but somebody developed high fins on platies; and the fish to the right is a highfinned platy. Photo by Dr. J. Norton.

There are several strains of albino swordtails. A deep red strain and the pale yellow strain shown here. Additionally this swordtail is what we call a lyretail because of the extended dorsal, anal and caudal fins. The long anal makes breeding almost impossible. Photo by the author.

THE ODD-BALLS

One of the reedfish to be kept in the aquarium is *Polypterus bichir* from Africa. It grows to 2½ feet in length. Photo by Klaus Paysan.

Toxotes chatareus is one of the archerfishes; it lives in brackish water in the Pacific and Indian Ocean areas. Photo by Marcuse.

Tetraodon palembangensis is a puffer which does very well in fresh water, though they are not good aquarium fish. Photo by Hansen.

THE ODD-BALLS

When the fish collector goes into the jungle for the "money fish" he collects a lot of "trash fish" along with them. Obviously, once having spent the money for the collecting trip, he discards as few fishes as possible, hoping there will be a market for some of the lesser known or less desirable species he collects. No one would buy "trash fish," so the label is changed to "odd-balls."

We might define an odd-ball as a fish which is unbreedable or less colorful or more aggressive than the more regular aquarium species and brought into the market in very limited quantities. Of course there are many odd-balls which might not be so termed. . . and there certainly are many highly colorful and peaceful species among them.

Many of the odd-balls are fishes which were, in the grand old days before World War II, almost all brought in by boat. Then a sailor could dip his nets into the nearest fresh water to the port of call in which his boat happened to be berthed at the time and, keeping everything small enough to fit into his shipboard aquarium, haul the fish back to Europe or America hoping to make some money with his rare cargo. This was a surprisingly rewarding hobby for many sailors, and it gave them something to do on the long ocean journeys. From this source quite a few brackish water species were often collected, especially from southeast Asia where scats, monodactylids and glassfish were always easy to catch, easy to keep and easy to sell. Sailors that made it to Africa often brought back colorful rivulins and annual fishes which are always to be found in small pools near busy seaports.

But as fish collecting got to be a bigger business and jet aircraft brought fishes to large European and American cities within hours of their swimming in jungle streams, the flow of odd-balls diminished until now an odd-ball is rather hard to find.

Chonerhinus naritus is a beautiful puffer for the freshwater tank. Photo by Elias.

Nematocentrus macculochi, one of the Australian rainbowfishes. Photo by S. Frank.

Bedotia geayi, a gorgeous fish from Madagascar. Photo by Dr. Herbert R. Axelrod.

I photographed these interesting fish in Australia. They live in brackish as well as marine water, and aquarists can successfully keep them in hard fresh water. They are *Scatophagus argus*, a widely distributed species. Their name translates into excrement-eater, which they earned by scavenging the over-the-water outhouses so common in the southeast Asian port cities.

I have used this section of the book to present many fishes which fall into categories basically too small to make major categories. Certainly whole books have been written about rivulins and many more books could. . . and should. . . have been written about the mormyrids of Africa and the knifefishes of both Africa and South America. Hopefully, if this present series of books is successful I'll be able to devote more space and more photographs to some of these interesting odd-balls.

Take the electric eels, the various electric catfishes and the many gymnotids. Certainly the thousands of hours being spent by highly respectable scientists inquiring into the source and reason for these discharges should result in a huge body of knowledge about these suitable aquarium inhabitants, more than enough to fill a good-sized book.

Then, too, the scats and monodactylids which range from southeast Asia to Australia to western Africa, though they have been imported by the millions by now, have been spawned only very rarely. Aquarists have a golden opportunity with these brackish water beauties.

The next time you visit a pet shop and see something which might not be common, and you have an empty tank, buy it. If you can photograph it as it grows and study its habits, what it eats, how it swims, when are its periods of activity. . . then write about it in a suitable aquarium magazine. And don't forget, when it dies, preserve the corpse so you can send it to an ichthyologist and get a proper identification.

The golden batfish, *Monodactylus argenteus*, photographed by the author in Taronga Zoo, Sydney, Australia. Most of these fish are silver.

Monodactylus sebae were collected by the author for the aquarium trade during the late 1950's in the Cameroons. They did well in either pure fresh water or pure salt water. Photo by the author.

From brackish water areas of southeast Asia come the glassfishes, known variously as *Ambassis* or *Chanda*. Different geographical races have more or less transparency. These fish do best in very hard water and are bred in outdoor pools in Florida. Photo by Dr. Stanislav Frank.

From the Celebes Islands comes this special kind of glassfish know as *Telmatherina ladigesi*, named in honor of Dr. Ladiges, a German ichthyologist who has an interest in aquarium fishes. Photo by Dr. Karl Knaack.

The famous electric eel, *Electrophorus electricus* from South America, is supposed to be powerful enough to shock and kill a 75-pound child. This is a must fish for the public aquarium, but it's a no-no for the home aquarist. Photo by Klaus Paysan.

The lungfishes are living fossils found in Africa, South America and Australia, though with different families on each continent. The fish shown here is from South Africa and has been identified as *Protopterus annectens*. There are about six different lungfishes, with about four being found in Africa. Photo by the author.

Snakeheads are not very interesting or desirable fishes for the home aquarist, but if you want an odd-ball, this is the kind of fish to get. This shows a small specimen of *Channa micropeltes*. Photo by Aaron Norman.

Africa has some weird-looking oddballs which are generally lumped under the names elephant noses, baby whales, trumpet faces, etc. Scientists recognize this group and refer to them usually as mormyrids. The fish shown to the left is *Gnathonemus macrolepidotus*, while the fish below may be *Marcusenius isidori*. Photos by the author.

Gnathonemus curvirostris (?) may be the name of this beast from Africa. It gives off electrical discharges which, some scientists say, are an effective means of communication. Photo by Klaus Paysan.

Xenomystus nigri is a rare knifefish which also gives off electrical impulses of interest to certain other fishes and most scientists! Photo by Klaus Paysan.

This *Gnathonemus* species, close to *Gnathonemus petersi*, has a weird mouthpiece which serves well in poking up the bottom for worms. The two knifefish in the background are *Xenomystus*. Photo by Klaus Paysan.

This fish was collected in the Rio Negro, Brazil and is supposed to be *Synbranchus marmoratus*. I doubt the identification, but for those with 12 feet long tanks who want a real odd-ball, this is it! Almost nothing is known about this fish. No one knows where it fits into the scheme of things evolutionary-wise. It looks like an eel but is not at all related to the true eels. It is friendly to handle and doesn't wriggle or bite. Photo by the author.

Black and yellow, small and equipped with suckerdisks which allow it to cling to almost any surface. . . that's *Brachygobius*, a genus of bumblebee fishes from southeast Asia. They are not usually long-lived in the aquarium. Photo by G.J.M. Timmerman.

Badis badis, a popular odd-ball. Photo by Hansen.

Osteoglossum bicirrhosum is a very odd fish. This may not be *O. bicirrhosum*, but the black aruana, *Osteoglossum ferreirai*. Photo by Aaron Norman of a young specimen.

A pair of weird odd-ball fish known as the leaf fish. Look closely and you can see them tending their eggs which they attached underneath the leaf. Photo by Hans Joachim Richter.

Africa has some very small and highly colorful fishes which are generally called rivulins. The males are more highly colored and with longer fins than females, with but very few exceptions. Here is a male *Aphyosemion filamentosum* dancing before another fish. Photo by Col. Scheel.

Aphyosemion bivittatum. This photo is from the cover of Col. Scheel's huge book called *Rivulins of the Old World*. It shows two males fighting.

Aphyosemion oeseri. Photo by E. Roloff.

Roloffia occidentalis male. Photo by Rudolf Zukal.

Aphyosemion walkeri male. Photo by Elek.

Aplocheilus panchax, found throughout southeast Asia. Photo by Hansen.

Aphyosemion sjoestedti. A male with the female swimming in the background. Photo by G.J.M. Timmerman.

Roloffia chaytori. Photo by V. Elek.

Austrofundulus dolichopterus, one of the most rare rivulins in the aquarium world. No one has been able to produce them for any length of time.

The author went to Brazil on the advice of the late General Thomas White, Chief of Staff of the U.S. Air Force, to find this fish named in his honor, *Cynolebias whitei*. The range of the fish is restricted to a few small holes in a cattle field about 100 miles outside Rio de Janeiro, Brazil. This is a mature male. Photo by Hans Joachim Richter.

A pair of spawning *Cynolebias whitei*. The male is much larger and more colorful than the female. They bury their eggs in the bottom of the tank. Photo by Hans Joachim Richter.

From Argentina come the several species we call the Argentine pearlfish. The fish to the right is *Cynolebias bellotti*, while the fish shown below is *Cynolebias nigripinnis*. Photos by Hansen and Zukal.

Aplocheilus lineatus from southeast Asia. Photo by Hansen.

A beautiful female *Aplocheilichthys katangae*. Photo by the author.

Aplocheilichthys flavipinnis, one of the lamp-eyes from Africa, has never become an aquarium favorite. Photo by Klaus Paysan.

Epiplatys chevalieri. Photo by Col. J. Scheel.

Epiplatys longiventralis male. Photo by Col. J. Scheel.

The most sought after rivulin, *Epiplatys annulatus*. The male is the upper fish in this famous photo taken by E. Roloff.

The Flordia flag fish, *Jordanella floridae*, as the male pushes the female into the gravel in their usual spawning ritual. Photo by V. Elek.

Epiplatys dageti, the firemouth panchax. This young male is not in full color. Photo by Dr. Stanislav Frank.

One of America's common bait-fishes is the killie *Fundulus chrysotus*. Photo by the author of a pair. The male is the lower fish.

In the lower half of Africa can be found a genus of very highly colorful fishes whose lives last less than a year. These are called annual fishes, and they live in water holes that dry out completely during the dry season. The fish above are *Nothobranchius rachovi*; they have just laid a few eggs in the mat of artificial dirt. Photo by Hans Joachim Richter.

This series of three photographs shows the annual fish *Nothobranchius rachovi* in its spawning role. In Africa the fish must lay their eggs during the rainy season because they all die when the water dries out. The eggs are laid in the mud, where they develop slowly until it rains again. Then the eggs hatch and the fry develop very quickly so they can spawn again before it dries out. The male, in the lower photo, forces the female into the bottom with his dorsal draped over her back. Photos by Richter.

A related species to *Nothobranchius rachovi* is the fire killie, *Nothobranchius palmquisti*. The female, as seen in the photo above, is very plain, while the male shown in the photograph below is full of color. Photos by Hans Joachim Richter.

A pair of *Rivulus holmiae*, a South American rivulin. Photo of a pair by Rudolf Zukal.

South America also houses *Pterolebias longipinnis*. This male is a rather poor example of how truly beautiful this species gets. Photo by Hans Joachim Richter.

INDEX

Page numbers in **bold** face refer to photographs

A

B

C